NEW JERUSALEM,

THE HEART OF THE BIBLE

DAROLD MEYER

COPYRIGHT © 2024 BY DAROLD MEYER

All rights reserved. This book or any portion thereof may not be reproduced or used in any manner whatsoever without the express written permission of the author except for the use of brief quotations in a book review.

Scripture quotations taken from the New American Standard Bible®, Copyright © 1960, 1962, 1963, 1968, 1971, 1972, 1973, 1975, 1977, 1995 by The Lockman Foundation Used by permission." (www.Lockman.org)

APPRECIATION

Dear Lord, Just like the previous books, I hope that this one is what You intended. By faith I will accept that it is, even though I am certain that it is not perfect, seeing as this vessel is not perfect. Thank You for Your grace; it **is** amazing.

My dear wife – When I wrote the first book, we were a few years away from 50 years together, but now I can say we are GOLDEN! Thank you for your love and putting up with Grumpy. Thank the Lord for giving us these years together. Let us finish our race!

John Boughan – John, thank you again for your help. I have enjoyed your fellowship while working on these three books.

All the Lord's saints – Thank You, Lord, for Your church. We are the continuance of Your life that has been flowing from generation to generation since the day You breathed on the first ones and said, "Receive the Holy Spirit." Now, with the help of Your faithful ones, I have received insight that helped me to write this book. May this also contribute to the understanding of those who seek it.

OTHER BOOKS BY THE AUTHOR

Run Your Race! - New Testament Warnings to Christians

The Christian life is described by the apostle Paul as a race, a race that we must run with endurance. While using different examples, Paul's exhortations perfectly echo those of Lord Jesus. With these exhortations came warnings, both from the Lord and from Paul, but these warnings are usually not applied to us in traditional teaching. Quite often great effort is made to deflect the warnings onto other people.

This book looks at all the warnings, every single one, that are present in the Gospels and in nearly every letter written by every New Testament author. There are far more than you probably realize. All are considered in their context to identify who it is that should be paying attention. If you have been born of the Spirit, if Christ is in you, then there is a race to run. When Christ appears, will we have confidence before Him, or will we shrink away in shame (1 John 2:28)?

Our One-Three God

Do you have trouble explaining what you believe about the trinity of the Godhead? Are you challenged when trying to explain to someone who disagrees with this understanding? This book can help you.

Each Person of our one-three God is considered in Scripture, including the uniqueness of each and the oneness of All.

We cannot understand Him according to our natural perspective, but God reveals Himself in the scriptures that He has provided to us. Even in appreciating what we see in God's revelation of Himself, we can only marvel and give Him praise and glory.

I hope this little book draws you into the Word and builds your faith.

NEW JERUSALEM, THE HEART OF THE BIBLE

Preface

"Come here, I will show you the bride, the wife of the Lamb."
(Revelation 21:9)

In my previous book, *Run Your Race! New Testament Warnings to Christians* (referred to hereafter as *RYR*) I mentioned the new Jerusalem several times. I feel that another book is warranted just on this topic, because the new Jerusalem is the goal that God is working toward, and it is at the heart of God's Word to us. It is the wonderful ending to God's long journey with man.

I have been telling anyone who asked, that my next book was going to be *New Jerusalem, The Bride*, but I could not get it started. I had the wrong approach...and no anointing. One cannot simply decide to write a book about the Bible. If a book is to be of God and from God, there **must** be an anointing. Jesus said, "Apart from Me you can do nothing" (John 15:5). Now I have peace to proceed, and with that peace an assurance that the anointing will carry this book along.

This is a book that is not merely a look at the features and highlights of this wonderful city, but a more complete work about how God, through His Son, by the Spirit, is building it. And why.

1 Corinthians 2:9 says, *but just as it is written, Things which eye has not seen and ear has not heard, and which has not entered the heart of man, all that God has prepared for those who love Him."* This is a wonderful verse. We hear it quoted often, but do you know what the next verse says? Verse 10 says, *For to us God revealed them through the Spirit; for the Spirit searches all things, even the depths of God.* Then verses 12-13a say, *Now we* **have** *received, not the spirit of the world, but the Spirit who is from God, so that we* **may know** *the things freely given to us by God, which things we also speak...*

Paul is saying that God has **already** revealed to us "all that God has prepared"! We **can** know it! I would agree that we have only a foretaste, but it is a foretaste of that which has been revealed. Are you waiting to go somewhere after death in order to find out? God has already revealed! The question is what **do** we see?

The new Jerusalem is our destiny, but maybe not in the way that you think. In this book we will look at God's Word without blinders and without the usual preconceptions. Are you ready? Can you open to the Spirit's speaking without reinterpreting what He says?

I hope that "Heart of the Bible" is an adequate term. I am referring to chapters 14 to 17 of John's gospel, **especially** chapter 14. Jesus is about to be betrayed, and He is spending the last remaining minutes that He has with His disciples, and finally (chapter 17) with His Father. Like any of us would do, He is telling them the most important things that remain to be said. The difference between Jesus and us is that the matters on His heart are so mysterious and so deep, that understanding them requires the rest of the Bible.

What do those four chapters have to do with the new Jerusalem? I will cover that in marvelous and wonderful detail!

Before we start, here are a few ground rules that I employ. 1] Scriptures are quoted from the New American Standard Bible 1995 edition. 2] Most direct quotes from the Bible will be in *italics,* without quotation marks. (Even though translators use italics to show words that have been added to aid interpretation, I will ignore that. If pointing out such an added word helps in the discussion, then it will be pointed out.) 3] Incomplete or partial quotes from the Bible might be enclosed in quotation marks instead of being italicized. 4] In order to not have to repeatedly say so, I now declare that **bolding** or any other form of emphasis used in quoting scripture is mine. 5] Any words that are presented as being from original language will be in *italics.*

My prayer and hope are that after reading this book, you will have a new appreciation for the city of the living God.

Chapters

1 The Vision	3
2 In the Beginning	5
3 The Picture	11
4 The Heart of the Bible	25
5 Betrothal	41
6 The Bride in the Old Testament	47
7 The Covenants	55
8 The Lord's Marriage	61
9 Parables	71
10 The Nations	77
11 The Habitation of God	81
12 The Spirit and the Bride	87
Scripture Index	93

The Vision

The first mention of the new Jerusalem in the book of Revelation occurs in chapter 3. In the letter to the church in Philadelphia, verse 12, the One walking among the lampstands says, *He who overcomes, I will make him a pillar in the temple of My God, and he will not go out from it anymore; and I will write on him the name of My God, and the name of the city of My God, the new Jerusalem, which comes down out of heaven from My God, and My new name.* The Lord says that the new Jerusalem is a city, that it comes down from heaven, and that it comes from God.

Notice that the name of the city will be written on the overcomer as a reward for faithfulness. Notice further that the name of this city is mentioned with God's name and Jesus's new name. That must be quite significant! What high company!

I will also point out that the new Jerusalem comes **down** out of heaven. This will be mentioned a few times.

We next see the new Jerusalem described as "the holy city" in chapter 21, verse 2. This is like no other city; it is set apart by God. It is again described as "coming down out of heaven from God." This city is for God and from God, and, as we will see later, it expresses God. What a marvelous city!

But verse 2 makes a new and wonderful point. This holy city is "made ready as a bride adorned for her husband." Wow! How beautiful is that?

I have heard others teach that the new Jerusalem is so beautiful that John is comparing it to a bride, but I think that understanding falls short of the reality. John is not making a comparison, but stating the fact that this city **is** the bride made ready to meet her husband. I say this with confidence because this is not the last word about the matter. John is not finished.

In verse 21:9 an angel says to John, *Come here, I will show you the bride, the wife of the Lamb.* Now we get a closer look at the city (the bride, the wife) first seen in verse 2. In verse 10 it is called "the holy city," and we are told for the **third** time that it is "coming down out of heaven from God." When the Holy Spirit repeats something, we need to pay attention! ...coming **down** ...coming **out** of heaven.

Chapters 21 and 22 give many more details, but at this early stage I simply want to help you begin to see that this holy city, the new Jerusalem, is a fit companion for her Husband.

Returning to an earlier point, verse 21:10 takes away the analogy of a city that is so beautiful that it compares to a bride, because now we know without any doubt that this **is** the bride! This city is even called the **wife** of the Lamb. I will show you the wife....and he showed me a city. Did the angel make a mistake? This reminds me of Revelation 5:5-6 where one of the elders told John to behold "the Lion that is from the tribe of Judah," but when John looked, he saw "a Lamb standing, as if slain." John seemingly saw something different from what he was told he was going to see, but in truth it was the same thing. The Lamb is the Lion. The city is the bride.

These three verses (2, 9, and 10) in chapter 21 should be enough to help us understand that this city is not heaven (it comes down **out** of heaven), and neither is it where all of our mansions will be. If you have read my first book (*RYR*), you know what's coming when I write about that. And, how many streets of gold are there, anyway?

In the Beginning

In every story there is a beginning and an end; a good story has a beginning that demands your attention; it has ebbs and flows, a climax, and a finish that helps you tie up loose ends. Our Bible, the story of God with man, has all of this.

The beginning of this story exhibits God's power and creativity, His divine order, and His attention to detail. He created the heavens and the earth and everything that lives. Every day's progress (except the second) resulted in a declaration of "good." Finally, on the sixth day, God made a man, and the whole work was declared by God to be "very good."

Verse 1:27 makes a general statement that makes it appear that God made man and woman at the same time. *God created man in His own image, in the image of God He created him; male and female He created them.* Chapter 2 has a recap of the sixth day beginning with verse 4. Here we see a more detailed explanation of what occurred on that day. God made Adam from the dust of the ground and planted a garden for him. Then God said (verse 18), *It is not good for the man to be alone; I will make a helper suitable for him.* What followed was an involved process that seems more complicated than it needed to be.

You might have heard in a message or two that in this part of the creation story, God is not talking about Adam and Eve only, but about Christ and the church. Let us review the reasons why this might be the case, because the implication is very significant. I suggest that this gets to the heart of the Bible.

God never does anything without reason. We need to get to His level to see, which is impossible for flesh and blood. But He gave us the Word, and we have the Spirit. So, why this involved process to give a wife to Adam? Each step shows us something in the life of Christ. First let us look at the plain text as it applies to Adam.

Strangely (to us, not to God) the first thing that God did was to bring the beasts and birds to Adam to see what he would call them. Children learn that Adam named the animals, but the deeper point is at the end of verse 2:20. *...but for Adam there was not found a* *helper suitable for him.* The main point was not in naming the animals, but to show us that Eve was to be more than special.

Having made this point, the next thing God did was to put Adam into a deep sleep and remove one of his ribs (verse 21). The next verse is interesting. It is a simple statement that from the rib God made a woman and brought her to Adam. *The Lord God fashioned into a woman the rib which He had taken from the man, and brought her to the man.*

The Hebrew word for "fashioned" is not the same as two other Hebrew words that are used in the first two chapters. Those two words are *bara* and *asah*. The first usually means to create as an original, initial work, and the second usually means to make from existing materials. It is not my intention to delve into those words, but to highlight this third word, *banah*.

Banah means to **build** something. Principal uses in the Old Testament refer to building a city, an altar, or a house (either a structure or a family). God **built** Eve, and now notice the difference between verses 2:20 and 2:23. Verse 20 ends with *but for Adam there was not found a helper suitable for him*. But after God presented Eve to Adam, his reaction was probably not the staid comment that we usually read into verse 23. Try to put some emotion into this verse: *This is **now** bone of **my** bones, and flesh of **my** flesh; she shall be called Woman because she was taken out of Man.* Again, with verse 20 as a backdrop, understand what Adam is saying: this time, this **one**, is very different from all the others that God had brought to him. Where the NASB says "this is now," other translations use expressions like "at last," or "this time."

Please do not say that I am comparing a woman to animals! This is the process that God chose, in order to make a point and to reveal His marvelous plan! In fact, even before He brought the animals to Adam (verse 19), God said (verse 18), *It is not good for the man to be alone; I will make him a helper suitable for him.* God could have made man and woman together, at the same time, but He did not. He could have omitted the step of Adam naming the animals, but He did not. God could have made Eve from the dust of ground, but

He did not. He did not do the ordinary things when it came to Eve. He did not follow the established patterns. Eve was so special!

And the point is that the woman, the wife, is a part of the husband, one with him in life and in nature. Even the phrase "a helper suitable for him" (verses 18 and 20) has the literal sense of "corresponding to." Eve corresponded to Adam! Do you see where this is going? God the Father has a wedding planned for His Son, but where is a suitable bride? A cow could never correspond to Adam, but Eve did. What bride can correspond to Christ?

How did this play out in the New Testament? Jesus was put to death on the cross. Adam's deep sleep corresponds to this. In the Lord's death the Roman soldier pierced His side with a spear, and blood and water poured out (John 19:34). God taking the rib from Adam corresponds to this. The mentioning of blood and water in that order is significant. The blood is for the forgiveness of our sins; the water (see Ephesians 5:25-26 below) is for our inward cleansing and sanctification.

Finally, we can see the building of Eve in the building of the church. This is brought out many times, especially in Paul's letters. In addition to the verses listed below, see also: Ephesians 5:23,27,29-30.

> Matthew 16:18 - *I also say to you that you are Peter, and upon this rock I will build My church*
> 1 Corinthians 3:9 - *For we are God's fellow workers; you are God's field, God's building.*
> 2 Corinthians 11:2 - *For I am jealous for you with a godly jealousy; for I betrothed you to one husband, so that to Christ I might present you as a pure virgin.*
> Ephesians 2:21-22 - *in whom the whole building, being fitted together, is growing into a holy temple in the Lord, in whom you also are being built together into a dwelling of God in the Spirit.*
> Ephesians 5:25-26 - *Husbands, love your wives, just as Christ also loved the church and gave Himself up for her, so that He might sanctify her, having cleansed her by the washing of water with the word*

Ephesians 5:32 - *This mystery is great; but I am speaking with reference to Christ and the church.*
1 Peter 2:5 - *you also, as living stones, are being built up as a spiritual house*
Revelation 21:2 - *And I saw the holy city, new Jerusalem, coming down out of heaven from God, made ready as a bride adorned for her husband.*

Now do you see that in order for the new Jerusalem to be the Lamb's wife, it must be something that comes from Him, corresponds to Him, matches Him in life and in nature, and is built by God? The above verses refer to the church. Is it a great leap from the church to the new Jerusalem? Remember that Revelation reveals the new Jerusalem to be the wife of the Lamb, and some of the above verses show the church to be exactly that.

I have already shown how the church came out of Christ by what happened on the cross after He died. How does the church fit the other requirements of corresponding to Him, matching Him, and being built by Him?

Perhaps the best way to show correspondence is to point out the move of the church and the local churches in the book of Acts. While that book has the title of the Acts of the Apostles, it is also the move of the Spirit in the church, as seen in the lives of the saints of those days. God did many things in many places through His church, even as He does to this day. Of course, we are not a perfect picture due to our fallen nature and the doggedness of our flesh, but at least we know that in the manifestation of God's kingdom we will fully correspond to Christ and be His perfect helper.

Does the church match Christ in His life and with His nature? Absolutely, even though imperfectly for the moment. This becomes more evident as we are constituted with more of the divine life through the long process of transformation. Peter described this well in his second letter, verses 1:2-3. *Grace and peace be multiplied to you in the knowledge of God and of Jesus our Lord; seeing that His divine power has granted to us everything pertaining to life and godliness, through the true knowledge of Him who called us by His own glory and excellence.* Peter concluded this thought in verse 4. *For by these He has granted to us His precious and magnificent promises, so that by them you may become **partakers** of the divine nature.* If this seems far from our reality now, I encourage you to not look at yourself (even though we do) but to look to the author and perfecter of our faith (Hebrews 12:2). This Perfecter will complete the work that He has begun in us (Philippians 1:6).

For the final point, the church being built by God, I refer you again to Matthew 16:18, John 2:19 and 21, 1 Corinthians 3:9, Ephesians 2:21-22, and Ephesians 4:12 and 16. All these show us that in this age God is in the business of building His church. With the same love and care that He built Eve, He is building the church, which is also the body of Christ and God's holy habitation.

But yet, one still might ask, "How is a **city** a match for the risen Lord? How can a city have the same life and nature as our Lord?" I hope that by the time you have finished this book, you will be able to see that this city is a **spiritual** habitation and that the Scriptures do support what I am saying. This discussion will begin in the next chapter.

That is what the divine story is all about, and I hope that you will appreciate and even get excited as we explore the details of the holy city.

The Picture

Before his fall Adam probably had brain function that greatly surpasses what we exhibit today, but he showed by his actions that he was very inferior to God and even the angels (being outsmarted by the fallen angel, Lucifer).

Nevertheless, God wanted to communicate with us and explain to us, especially in the church age, what He is doing, what is His goal, and how He is accomplishing His will. With the advantage of the New Testament we are able to see that many things in the Old Testament were written for our understanding, but could not have possibly been understood prior to the Lord's incarnation. Some things are obvious now: the three days and nights that Jonah spent in the fish, the bronze serpent that was raised on a pole. Jesus Himself mentioned these things, as well as a few others, referring to them as signs. Paul referred to Old Testament places and events as allegories (Galatians 4:24).

Some things are types (as in "typology"), and others are said to be shadows. Adam was a type of Christ. Paul wrote in Colossians 2:17 that the holy days and the sabbaths were shadows of the reality that is Christ Himself (see also Hebrews 10:1). The Old Testament has so many items and events that are types and shadows that enrich our understanding of the Father, the Son, the Holy Spirit, the church, and us individually. Our understanding of what Jesus accomplished as the Lamb of God is infinitely more than what is written in the Gospels.

Revelation is a book of unveiling, even as the first verse declares it to be "The Revelation of Jesus Christ." However, a lot of the unveiling is done through signs, which I sometimes like to call pictures. Many people are intimidated by some of these pictures (a dragon, a beast with seven heads, another beast with two horns, etc.), but these are pictures, representations of something. Just as a picture is worth a thousand words, these pictures reveal the nature of what the real thing is.

Revelation has pictures of positive things also. In the first chapter, verse 12, John sees seven golden lampstands. What are those? The Lord Himself tells John in verse 20 that they are the churches, the same seven churches to which Revelation is written. In the Lord's right hand are seven stars. Those are the angels, or messengers, of those churches. It is not that difficult then to understand these things as pictures. Chapter 14 also has pictures of the two harvests at the end of this age.

But, for some reason, the church fails to see the final vision for what it is...**a picture**. Saying that does not diminish the subject of the picture. On the contrary, the details reveal the marvelous and beautiful nature of the bride of the Lamb, the new Jerusalem!

While we try to understand the meanings of the other pictures in Revelation, the church does not do the same when it comes to this most important picture; instead, it latches onto the description as physical reality. The pretty picture took on its own reality, and we think we are going to walk on streets of gold.

The bride is announced in chapter 19, but before we see the bride, verses 1 through 4 sum up the destruction of another **woman**, another **city**, the great harlot Babylon. This city is depicted in chapter 17 as really despicable. Her description is given in verses 2 through 6, and then verse 17:18 says, *The woman whom you saw is the great city, which reigns over the kings of the earth*. This is a spiritual (albeit, evil) city that has been around for thousands of years, manifested in various ways through history as she persecuted God's people. You can find other books on the topic; my aim here is to point out the consistency of God's Word in presenting two spiritual entities (one evil, one holy) in similar ways. If the first is understood as an evil woman by means of a picture, then why not understand the second, especially when the second is **specifically** presented in that fashion? *I will show you the bride, the wife of the Lamb....and* [he] *showed me the holy city, Jerusalem* (21:9,10).

Revelation shows the culmination of many things, and among them are these two cities, these two women, the harlot and the bride. Two women, two cities, two pictures.

Coming back to chapter 19 we see that God first deals with the harlot. Her destruction is celebrated by the 24 elders and the four living creatures with "Amen. Hallelujah!"

But then, like a crescendo (verse 6), *I heard something like the voice of a great multitude and like the sound of many waters and like the sound of mighty peals of thunder....* Wow! Something **big** is coming.... The rest of verse 6 and verse 7 say, *"Hallelujah! For the Lord our God, the Almighty, reigns. Let us rejoice and be glad and give the glory to Him, for the marriage of the Lamb has come and His bride has made herself ready."*

And then what? Jesus returns! Verse 11 says, ...*And I saw heaven opened, and behold, a white horse, and He who sat on it is called Faithful and True, and in righteousness He judges and wages war.* Our Lord's return to this earth is tied to His bride's readiness. This is what is implied in 2 Peter 3:11b-12a, *what sort of people ought you to be in holy conduct and godliness, looking for and **hastening** the coming of the day of God.* There **is** a connection.

I grieve, and my heart aches whenever I am reminded about how much time I have wasted and lost. We want the Lord to return, and He **wants** to return, but how can there be a marriage supper without a bride who is ready? It is not that everybody is waiting for me or you, of course, but collectively we all need to be part of the bride that "has made herself ready."

But we must get back on topic, back to the picture. Most of Revelation chapter 21 and a good part of 22 describe the many aspects of the bride. These all mean something, and their significance will become apparent.

The first thing that John saw was the bride's glory and brilliance (21:11). ....*having the glory of God. Her brilliance was like a very costly stone, as a stone of crystal-clear jasper.* This city, the bride, expresses God! This is the first characteristic that has a spiritual connotation. You will find other translations that use "light" or "radiance" for brilliance. The Greek word, *phoster*, is used one other time, in Philippians 2:15: ....*so that you will prove yourselves to be blameless and innocent, children of God above reproach in the midst of a crooked and perverse generation, among whom you appear as **lights** in the world.*

Another, more common, Greek word for light is *phos*. I want to point out that both Jesus and we are this light. Jesus said several times that He is the light of the world (John 8:12, 9:5, 12:46). John 9:5 says, *While I am in the world, I am the Light of the world.* But He also said, **You** *are the light of the world. A city set on a hill cannot be hidden* (Matthew 5:14). The source of our light is not from ourselves, but from Him. And so, while the bride is not the source of light, the source is within her. As it is now, so it will be then! We are light; the city is light, and we are the city.

This is our first example, and while one example certainly cannot prove a case, I will point out over and over that the realities of the new Jerusalem are our realities **today**. Of course, today we have our fallen nature and the flesh, so the characteristics that we see in the bride are muted now, but what we are shown in Revelation is what can be our experience during this life. So, in this characteristic we are to be God's lights in this world, and so it will be for eternity.

(A quick note: I think it would be boring to read about every detail, and I do not have a lot to say about some, so please forgive me if I skip over something that you might have wanted me to cover.)

Next we notice the wall and the gates (21:12-14). The wall shows the built up church, especially those brothers and sisters that the Lord has put us with. We protect each other. If we allow satan (I will not capitalize that name) to separate us from fellowship, we become easy prey for his schemes. A very good example of this application is Paul. Of all the letters that we have, only his first letter to Timothy is written without a reference to another brother being with him. He was with brothers in his travels and in his communications. This shows Paul's connection with the wall.

The wall has twelve foundation stones. The names of the twelve apostles are written on them. This was the start of the building of this city, the bride, and the building work continues until the bride makes herself ready.

There are twelve gates, and names of the twelve tribes of Israel are written on them. This shows that the bride includes God's faithful who lived before Jesus was born. God will not forget about His promises to Israel. Yes, they will physically occupy the land that God promised to Abraham, with the literal city Jerusalem, but they will also be included in the spiritual bride.

The gates are interesting. Each is a pearl, and this shows God's wonderful love and forgiveness for His chosen people. In *RYR* I wrote a chapter in the appendix about Making Pearls. In short, a pearl is created when a clam or oyster is wounded by a grain of sand or other intrusion. A secretion covers the wound and something beautiful is created. This is the basis for our entrance into the city.

Even though the gates have the names of the tribes of Israel, in this church age Israel cannot function as gates to the city. I see elders and others who labor with them as our gates. Paul's exhortation to the Ephesian elders shows the protection that a gate provides. Notice what Paul said to the elders. *Be on guard for yourselves and for all the flock, among which the Holy Spirit has made you overseers, to shepherd the church of God which He purchased with His own blood. I know that after my departure savage wolves will come in among you, not sparing the flock; and from among your own selves men will arise, speaking perverse things, to draw away the disciples after them. Therefore be on the alert,....*(Acts 20:28-31a). Compare this to Revelation 21:27, which says, *and nothing unclean, and no one who practices abomination and lying, shall ever come into it.* Verse 22:15 has an additional list of disqualifications.

What happens when the gates fail? Paul has to write certain letters to the churches, and Jesus has to dictate letters "to the seven churches that are in Asia" (Revelation 1:4 and chapters 2 and 3). The evil influences come in and corrupt the gospel, distract and damage the saints, and bring our Shepherd's displeasure. Our church leaders need our prayers.

How are the gates applicable to the next age? Since they are part of this picture of the bride, what is their significance? I do not think that I have a complete understanding, but it is stated in verse 21:25 that the gates will never be closed. Besides being for protection, gates, when they are open, are centers of activity and commerce. Look at verses 21:24 and 26. *The nations will walk by its light, and the kings of the earth will bring their glory into it. ....and they will bring the glory and the honor of the nations into it.* Compare this to Isaiah 60:1-3. *Arise, shine; for your light has come, And the glory of the LORD has risen upon you. For behold, darkness will cover the earth And deep darkness the peoples; But the LORD will rise upon you And His glory will appear upon you. Nations will come to your light, And kings to the brightness of your rising.* The light in verse 21:24 of Revelation is spiritual light. The Lord and we will be the light of the world in fulness. There will be true peace, real security, and eternal light.

The last feature that I want to cover in chapter 21 is the street in verse 21. How many streets of gold are there? One. **Only** one. "Street" is singular. Streets (plural) could be expected in a physical city, but since we are talking about a picture of the wife of the Lamb, there must be a reason for there being only one. This street goes to God. It is the way of life, the divine life. The Greek word used for this life is *zoe*. There is no other street. Jesus is the only way to the Father, but we are not waiting for some future day to come to the Father. Jesus is our way **now**. We have come to the Father **already** by believing into the name of our Savior. As it is now, so it will be then.

Now in chapter 22 of Revelation let us look at the river. *Then he showed me a river of the water of life, clear as crystal, coming from the throne of God and of the Lamb* (verse 22:1). We saw that the street is our way to God; now we see God coming to man. This river flows from God and the Lamb, bringing the divine (*zoe*) life to us.

John gave us two illustrations of this river in his gospel, each showing a particular purpose. The first is in chapter 4 when Jesus met the Samaritan woman at the well. Verse 10 says, *Jesus answered and said to her, "If you knew the gift of God, and who it is who says to you, 'Give Me a drink,' you would have asked Him, and He would have given you living water."* The Lamb of God is the source of the water of life. Jesus emphasized the point in verse 14. *But whoever drinks of the water that I will give him shall never thirst; but the water that I will give him will become in him a well of water springing up to eternal life.*

In the context of the Lord's conversation with the sinful woman, I believe that this well of water is for the transformation of our soul. The living water from God is received by our spirit, and from there it springs up to eternal life to renew us from within. This was the need of the sinful woman .... and all of us.

John's second mention is in chapter 7. *Now on the last day, the great day of the feast, Jesus stood and cried out, saying, "If anyone is thirsty, let him come to Me and drink. He who believes in Me, as the Scripture said, 'From his innermost being will flow rivers of living water.'"* (7:37-38) The living water comes to us to satisfy our thirst, but in this illustration, I think the Lord is showing us that this river of life is not for us only, but that it will flow out to others, thus bringing the divine life to them: salvation for unbelievers and fellowship with God's people.

The eternal life flows now from God to us, and from us to others. The gospel will not be preached in the next age, but we will always have the divine life flowing into and out of us. Our fellowship of life will be magnified and forever enjoyed. As it is now, so it will be then!

I think it is significant that the river is in the middle of the street. This shows the continuous interaction between God and His people. As we approach the Father, even the throne of grace, we are supplied by the river! This is a wonderful picture!

Not only is there a river, but on both sides of the river the tree of life grows. While we are in fellowship with God, we enjoy the tree of life, just as God intended in the garden of Eden. But how does one tree grow on both sides of the one river? I have heard it described as a vine, as in "I am the vine, you are the branches" from John 15:5. That would help to visualize the matter, but the Greek word for vine is *ampelos*, and the word for tree is *xylon*. The word used in Revelation 22:2 is *xylon*, so I think "tree" is correct. What did John see? Physically, that is beyond my ability to comprehend, but as a spiritual matter, there is no problem. We have Christ as our tree of life now, and we will have Christ as our tree of life for eternity. Verse 22:14 even says, *Blessed are those who wash their robes, so that they may have the right to the tree of life.* One more time... As it is now, so it will always be!

This tree of life produces fruit, twelve kinds. *On either side of the river was the tree of life, bearing twelve kinds of fruit, yielding its fruit every month* (verse 22:2). I believe that most have the understanding (well, I did) that this means that this month it bears apples, next month pears, and then oranges. But I think God is not limited in this way. One day I realized that **all** the various fruits (whatever they are) could be produced every month! How about that?

But wait! Some years later, I realized that even that kind of thinking (apples, pears, oranges) places the tree of life in the physical realm. If this is a picture of something spiritual, then what is God showing us? Galatians 5:22-23a might offer a hint. *But the **fruit** of the Spirit is love, joy, peace, patience, kindness, goodness, faithfulness, gentleness, self-control.* Here are few others:

> John 4:36 - *Already he who reaps is receiving wages and is gathering **fruit** for life eternal*
> Romans 7:4 - *so that you might be joined to another, to Him who was raised from the dead, in order that we might bear **fruit** for God*
> Ephesians 5:8-9 - *for you were formerly darkness, but now you are Light in the Lord; walk as children of Light (for the **fruit** of the Light consists in all goodness and righteousness and truth)*
> Hebrews 12:11 - *All discipline for the moment seems not to be joyful, but sorrowful; yet to those who have been trained by it, afterwards it yields the peaceful **fruit** of righteousness.*

The Holy Spirit is producing life's fruit in us now, and it will not stop. For eternity we will enjoy the fruit that has been, and is being, produced in us now, and the same fruit that will be produced even then! As it is now, so it will always be! God is limitless, and our experience of Him will be unlimited. Everything that hinders us now will be removed. I can't wait for that!

There is one more aspect of the tree. The last part of verse 22:2 says, *and the leaves of the tree were for the healing of the nations.* Wait a minute...what nations? I discussed this matter in detail in *RYR*, but I hope this brief explanation might be sufficient. Remember, God's Word is true, and it does not conform itself to what we want it to say. I try to be mindful of that even as I write this book. The Word says that there will be nations, even after the Lord's return. Not only are the nations mentioned here in verse 22:2, but previously in verses 21:24 and 26. *The **nations** will walk by its light, and the **kings** of the earth will bring their glory into it. .... and they will bring the glory and the honor of the **nations** into it.* Notice that I highlighted "kings." Were we not told that the nations will be ruled by us with a rod of iron? Well, here they are! Remember, this is not heaven. This is the earth, where Jesus (and the prophets) said He would establish His kingdom.

So now, back to the leaves. If we take the picture of the new Jerusalem as a physical city, then how would the leaves be used? Would they have medicinal properties for physical healing? Will that heal the heart? I will give you my understanding of a **spiritual** application of this picture. I hope it is clear enough.

Jesus identified Israel with the fig tree in Matthew 24:32-35, Mark 13:28-31, and Luke 13:6-9. Matthew and Mark read the same: *Now learn the parable from the fig tree: when its branch has already become tender and **puts forth its leaves**, you know that summer is near.* One day, while reading with my wife *The Pursuit of God* by A. W. Tozer, I realized why Adam and Eve used **fig leaves** to cover themselves. Just a coincidence? There is no such thing in God's Word. When we feel uncomfortable before God, we often try to hide ourselves behind religion. That is what we see way back in Genesis. We hope that religion, Jewish religion when Jesus walked among us and Christian religion now, will appease our conscience before God. What was God's solution for the fig leaves? He killed a Lamb.

What is the Jewish religion? The law. When Jesus looked for fruit on the fig tree (Matthew 21:19 and Mark 11:13), He found nothing but religion. There was no fruit for man or God, nothing enjoyable, no life.

Now, let us bring this back to the new Jerusalem. "Wait! Are you going to tell me that the nations are to be healed by the law? The healing by the leaves of the tree of life is by the law?" This is where the Old Testament can help us. Isaiah 2:2-3 and Micah 4:1-2 are very similar passages. This is from Micah:

> *And it will come about in the last days*
> *That the mountain of the house of the LORD*
> *Will be established as the chief of the mountains.*
> *It will be raised above the hills,*
> *And the peoples will stream to it.*
> *Many nations will come and say,*
> *"Come and let us go up to the mountain of the LORD*
> *And to the house of the God of Jacob,*
> *That He may **teach us** about His ways*
> *And that we may walk in His paths."*
> *For from Zion will go forth the **law**,*
> *Even the word of the LORD from Jerusalem.*

We are witnesses to what happens when societies ignore God, try to remove everything that reminds them of God, and throw off every restraint of civility. Even though we hope that all will come to Christ for salvation, the law of God serves to guide us and to protect us and society until the moment comes. In Galatians 3:24 Paul wrote, *Therefore the Law has become our tutor to lead us to Christ.*

When Christ sets up His kingdom on this earth, He will not be ignored. All nations will be continually reminded by us who will rule them. Zechariah 14:16-17 shows us that the Feast of Tabernacles (booths in the NASB) will be extended to the nations, but it will also be a requirement. *Then it will come about that any who are left of all the nations that went against Jerusalem will go up from year to year to worship the King, the LORD of hosts, and to celebrate the Feast of Booths. And it will be that whichever of the families of the earth does not go up to Jerusalem to worship the King, the LORD of hosts, there will be no rain on them.* I do not know if the nations will build booths as the Israelites did, but they will surely receive an annual reminder of who is in charge. More positively, they will receive instruction on how to live in peace and love. Micah 4:2 seems to support this.

Many nations will come and say,
Come and let us go up to the mountain of the LORD
And to the house of the God of Jacob,
*That He may **teach us about His ways***
*And that we may **walk in His paths.***
For from Zion will go forth the law,
Even the word of the LORD from Jerusalem.

But I remind you what Zechariah 14:16 says. *Then it will come about that any who are left of all the nations that **went against** Jerusalem...* Among the nations will be those who will have fought against God and Israel at the end of this age. Is it any wonder that a little "iron" will be required? But the goal will be for their healing. Can you imagine how blessed those people will feel? They will have survived the end of this age, and now they will experience restoration, peace, and even love through the healing that will come from the leaves of the tree of life.

Here I will take a moment to clarify something about ruling the nations. The Greek word for "ruling" is *poimaino*, and it is used eleven times in the New Testament. It is only in Revelation that the translators give it the sense of ruling. Revelation 19:15, for instance, says, *From His mouth comes a sharp sword, so that with it He may strike down the nations, and He will rule them with a rod of iron.* However, six times from Matthew to 1 Peter, *poimaino* refers to shepherding sheep. Jude 1:12 speaks of those who selfishly "care for themselves," using that word. If we think of shepherding the nations, that helps to give a different perspective. After all, when Jesus walked this earth, did He not say that lording it over others was **not** His way, and that it will not be ours? We might then carry the title of kings, but we will be shepherds. Our rod might be iron, but we will be shepherds.

What the Prophets Saw

You might be wondering about the vision of the temple in chapters 40, 47, and 48 of Ezekiel. There are differences between what Ezekiel saw and the vision of the new Jerusalem. Ezekiel's vision focused on the temple; and according to Revelation 21:22, John saw **no** temple in the new Jerusalem. *I saw no temple in it, for the Lord God the Almighty and the Lamb are its temple.*

In Ezekiel 47 we see a river flowing from the temple. It is an ever-deepening river, full of life. It flows from the temple, and it eventually reaches the Dead Sea. This river even freshens the water of the Dead Sea and brings life into it. Here is verse 47:9. *It will come about that every living creature which swarms in every place where the river goes, will live. And there will be very many fish, for these waters go there and the others become fresh; so everything will live where the river goes.*

Ezekiel saw a future physical temple in the land that God promised to Israel. Ezekiel 48 then shows how the land will be apportioned to the tribes. This chapter also gives us the dimensions of the city, the earthly Jerusalem, a little over 1.25 miles on each side (4500 cubits according to 48:30-34). There will be a physical city, and there will be (already is) a spiritual.

These chapters in Ezekiel can certainly be applied to us as an allegory. There is much that can be said as the river relates to our walk with the Lord. Paul applied the Old Testament in this way. Nevertheless, Ezekiel saw something that **will** exist in the next age.

What about Isaiah? The visions that he saw bear the same features as John wrote in Revelation. Check out verses 54:11-12, 60:11, 60:14, 60:19, and 65:17. Did Isaiah see a physical city, or did he see a spiritual city?

When I have questions like this, I review what is known. More importantly, I ask, seek, and knock. The Lord's revelation of what is true is more important than a point that I am trying to make. I want His truth, not what I think it should be.

It has been said that the New Testament is concealed in the Old, and that the Old Testament is revealed in the New. Isaiah saw a city in different aspects, written mainly in the chapters listed above. In this case the Old Testament is revealed in the New in the book of Revelation. And what do we know from Revelation? *"Come here, I will show you the bride, the wife of the Lamb."* ...*and [he] showed me the holy city, Jerusalem, coming down out of heaven from God* (Revelation 21:9b,10b). We have covered this. This is the governing verse for identifying the new Jerusalem. Therefore, it seems to me that Isaiah's visions of Jerusalem were the same vision of the bride!

In this chapter we looked at the new Jerusalem's brilliance and glory; her walls, foundation, and gates; and the street, the river, the tree of life, and the tree's leaves. I hope that what was presented is clear enough to help you realize that these aspects of the holy city have real application in our lives and in the next age. The Lord presented this picture, the last of many pictures, not for us to get side-tracked by the picture, but to see the revelation of the bride!

A final point. Since we should take the Bible literally as much as possible, some therefore say that the description of the bride must surely be literal. The problem then is that there is a problem. I do not want to repeat the entire chapter here, but what do you do with verse 21:9? *I will show you the bride, the wife of the Lamb.* I take **this** verse literally. It then follows that the description of the bride is figurative. Both cannot be literal; it is one or the other. Is the Lamb marrying His people, or is He marrying a huge cube? The answer gets to the heart of the Bible.

The Heart of the Bible

I wrote about John 14 in *RYR* and in *Our One-Three God*. Even if you have read those books, please do not skip this chapter. There will be repetition, but also new insights. Besides, it never hurts us to hear something more than once.

Jesus was quite clear in saying that He was going away and that His going was to the Father. An important question to answer is, **when** did He go to the Father? Even though I know that many will point to the Lord's ascension in Acts 1 as the moment when He fulfilled that statement, I was caught off-guard a few years ago by the thought that John 20:22 was a **symbolic** act. John 20:22 says this: *And when He had said this, He breathed on them and said to them, "Receive the Holy Spirit."* The reasoning was that He had resurrected, but not yet ascended, so therefore verse 22 could not be describing a real receiving of the Holy Spirit. I had not thought of that before. It would have **had** to be a symbolic act, if the Lord had not yet ascended to the Father.

On the other hand, I am convinced that the resurrected Lord's ascension to the Father is concealed and revealed in chapter 20. We will get into this later, but I mention this now to make the following point. This is an illustration of how an understanding of one passage can influence the understanding of another. At times this has significant implications. This is why, when coming to the Word, we should have an attitude of openness to the Lord, ready to receive His speaking, regardless of current or long held understandings.

Since before *RYR* was published, I have had some unanswered questions. For sure, I received a lot of light and understanding as I wrote that book, and I have continued to ask the Lord for revelation and understanding. Some of that will be in evidence in this work.

So, let's get into chapter 14, but know that chapter 14 does not begin with verse 1. In the original manuscripts there were no chapters. Chapters were added to the New Testament in 1227 by Stephen Langton, an archbishop of Canterbury. Verses were numbered in the OT and the NT about 200 hundred and 300 years later, respectively.

To begin to understand chapter 14, we need to back up to chapter 13. Jesus began at verse 13:33 to unveil His departure. *Little children, I am with you a little longer. You will seek Me; and as I said to the Jews, now I also say to you, 'Where I am going, you cannot come.'* Again, in verse 36 Jesus said in answer to Peter, *Where I go, you cannot follow Me now; but you will follow later.* In response to this, Peter said his famous, *Lord, why can I not follow You right now? I will lay down my life for You* (verse 37). Jesus' more famous reply was *Will you lay down your life for Me? Truly, truly, I say to you, a rooster will not crow until you deny Me three times* (verse 38).

Without the limitation of the chapter division, let us read verses 13:38 and 14:1. *Jesus answered, "Will you lay down your life for Me? Truly, truly, I say to you, a rooster will not crow until you deny Me three times. Do not let your heart be troubled; believe in God, believe also in Me.*

In this context let us now see the next **very** famous verse: *In My Father's house are many dwelling places* [mansions]; *if it were not so, I would have told you; for I go to prepare a place for you.* I am not going to pretend that Peter and the other disciples understood that, but suppose they understood it to mean what you might have been taught, that Jesus was going to the Father's house in heaven to build a mansion or similar nice house. Do you really think that was going to help them to feel better about the situation they were beginning to comprehend? Would they be that shallow? Would Jesus be that shallow? I think not! But this shallow teaching was introduced into the church, and it is so accepted that you can find the idea of mansions in many songs.

Now that I have offended you to no end, let us look into this chapter to see what God's heart is. John 14 is my favorite chapter because of what it reveals. Even if it is already your favorite chapter, it can be still, but for a deeper reason. Please stay with me.

In verse 2 there are two words that we need to understand: house and mansions (according to KJV). The first word has a unique NT definition, and the second has a definition that is to be found within the context of this same chapter 14.

The Greek word for "house" in this verse is *oikia*. It is primarily translated as "house," and by extension it includes the members of the household. There is another word in the NT, and that is *oikos*, which mainly refers to the household, but it is also translated as "house" more than 90% of the time. Why do I point out these two similar, but different words? It is because in many cases one word is used as if it had the definition of the other word, and vice versa. With this understanding as my permission, I will make the case that Jesus in verse 2 was in no way referring to heaven as the Father's house.

Greek	**Translated**	**Also**
Oikia	House	Household
Oikos	Household	House

Here are some verses where *oikia* is used, usually translated as "**house**":

> Matthew 7:24 - ...*may be compared to a wise man who built his **house** on the rock*
> Matthew 10:13 - *If the **house** is worthy, give it your blessing of peace.*
> Mark 3:25 - ...*If a **house** is divided against itself, that **house** will not be able to stand.*
> 1 Corinthians 16:15 - ...*you know the **household** of Stephanas, that they were the first fruits of Achaia*
> Philippeans 4:22 - *All the saints greet you, especially those of Caesar's **household**.*

Notice that I listed mostly verses that show that *oikia* can easily (and correctly) be understood as a house**hold** rather than a physical house.

Now here are verses that use *oikos*, primarily translated as "**household**":

> Luke 19:9 - ...*Today salvation has come to this **house***

> Luke 22:54 - *...they led Him away and brought Him to the **house** of the high priest*
> John 11:20 - *Martha therefore, when she heard that Jesus was coming, went to meet Him, but Mary stayed at the **house**.*
> Acts 2:36 - *Therefore let all the **house** of Israel know for certain...*
> Acts 10:2 - *a devout man, and one who feared God with all his **household***

Notice that Luke 22:54 and John 11:20 refer to a physical place, even though *oikos* means "household."

What is the point of all this? We must endeavor to handle the Word of God carefully. We need to resist the temptation to use a verse here and a verse there to prove a point that we want to make. In this case I will be trying to undo some things that you might have believed for all your life. That puts a double responsibility on me to be accurate, to speak only what the Word presents to us, and to **never** put forth something that is only an opinion.

The reason for presenting above that there are two words for house and household is that *oikia* (house) is used in John 14:2 (*In my Father's house*). Since *oikia* means house**hold** in many contexts, we cannot hang our hat on an understanding of "house."

However, there are direct New Testament references to God's house that use *oikos*. *Oikos* (household) is used in these following verses that are not listed above.

> 1 Timothy 3:15 - *but in case I am delayed, I write so that you will know how one ought to conduct himself in the **household** of God, which is the church of the living God, the pillar and support of the truth.*
> Hebrews 3:6 - *but Christ was faithful as a Son over His **house** —whose **house** we are, if we hold fast our confidence and the boast of our hope firm until the end.*

We are God's **household** and His **house**. This is God's New Testament economy. We are His family, and we are His home.

In fact, I will suggest that the idea of heaven being God's house is completely foreign to God's revelation in the Bible. As far as I have found, there are only three verses that might come close to suggesting that. They are 1 Kings 8:30, 39, and 43. *Listen to the supplication of Your servant and of Your people Israel, when they pray toward this place; hear in heaven Your dwelling place; hear and forgive.* Verse 39 also says, *then hear in heaven Your dwelling place.* "Dwelling place," is comprised of two Hebrew words, *yashab maqowm.* Neither word means "home" or "house." Out of 402 usages, *maqowm* is translated in the KJV as "home" only three times, and none of those refer to a dwelling for God. See 1 Samuel 2:20 and 2 Chronicles 25:10. The NASB translates *maqowm* as "home" in those same two verses plus four others with a note that the Hebrew word means "place." And again, none of the verses refer to God.

Other references to heaven as being a place of God, refer to heaven as God's **throne**. Here are three.

> Psalm 103:19 - *The LORD has established His **throne** in the heavens,...*
> Psalm 123:1 - *To You I lift up my eyes,*
> *O You who are **enthroned** in the heavens!*
> Isaiah 66:1 - *Heaven is My **throne** and the earth is My footstool.*

There are twenty verses in the NASB (22 in KJV) that contain both words, "heaven" and "house." While "heaven" is referred to in various contexts, "house" (Hebrew *bayit;* Greek *oikos*) refers to an **earthly** dwelling in every case! An example is 2 Chronicles, the end of verse 36:23. *He has appointed me to build Him a house in Jerusalem, which is in Judah.*

There are nearly 500 of references to "house of the Lord" or "house of God" on this earth, both as a building and as a household. There might be around ten references to God's earthly dwelling as a dwelling place (I do not shy away from inconvenient verses), but I find zero references to heaven as God's house.

Time after time God's house is associated with a habitation on earth, because He wants to be in a relationship with man. In the Old Testament the house was the tabernacle and the temple. Check out these verses.

> 1 Chronicles 17:12 - *He shall build for Me a **house**, and I will establish his throne forever.*
> Isaiah 56:7 - *...For My house will be called a **house** of prayer for all the peoples.*
> Jeremiah 12:7 - *I have forsaken My **house**...*
> Ezekiel 23:39 - *they entered My sanctuary on the same day to profane it; and lo, thus they did within My **house**.*
> Zechariah 1:16 - *...I will return to Jerusalem with compassion; My **house** will be built in it...*

The OT house is a type and a picture of the reality of God's NT house, the church.

> 1 Corinthians 3:17b - *For the temple of God is holy, and that is what **you** are.*
> 2 Corinthians 6:16a - *...For **we** are the temple of the living God.*
> Ephesians 2:21-22 - *In whom the whole **building**, being fitted together, is growing into a holy temple in the Lord, in whom **you** also are being built together into a dwelling of God in the Spirit.*
> 1 Timothy 3:15b - *The household of God, which is the **church** of the living God, the pillar and support of the truth.*

The rest of this book will not chase rabbit trails, but I feel the need to take this extra step to clearly show that Jesus in John 14:2 is absolutely **not** saying that His Father's house is heaven or in heaven. We, the church, are both God's house and His household. Properly understanding this chapter will provide a foundation to understanding what God is doing and what is on His heart.

If this is the correct way to understand John 14:2, then what about the "mansions" that Jesus mentioned? That word is the result of a very unfortunate translation in the KJV, and because of this, many of God's dear children have been cheated and even harmed.

The Greek word in verse 2 is *mone*, which simply means a dwelling place. "Okay, so I don't get a mansion, but surely Jesus would build me a nice house or a room, no matter the size!" Let me say clearly: Jesus is not talking about something **for** us; He is talking **about** us!

This Greek word *mone* is used in only one other place, and that happens to be in the same chapter. It is in verse 23, where Jesus said, *...If anyone loves Me, he will keep My word; and My Father will love him, and We will come to him and make Our **abode** with him.* It is absolutely arbitrary to translate *mone* as "abode" in one place and as "mansions" in another. I have heard several stories about how the KJV came to have "mansions" in the second verse, so I do not know which is correct. But the reason does not matter. The reality is that Jesus was talking about **us**!

Let us look again at something in chapter 13. In verse 13:18 Jesus said, *I do not speak of all of you. I know the ones I have chosen; but it is that the Scripture may be fulfilled, 'He who eats My bread has lifted up his heel against Me.'* Then verse 19: *From now on I am telling you before it comes to pass, so that when it does occur, you may believe that I am...* It is clear that Jesus is declaring an event before it comes to pass so that the disciples will believe Him and believe in Him when it is fulfilled.

Now I will set a trap. I do not mind telling you that it is a trap, because I am not trying to pull the wool over your eyes. We are on the same side. Do you know when, as recorded in John's gospel, Jesus made the same statement in telling the disciples about something before it comes to pass? We-e-l-ll, how about chapter 14? Verse 28 says, *You **heard** that I **said** to you, 'I go away, and I will come to you.'* When did Jesus say that? That would be verses 2 and 3! And then verse 29 says, *Now I have told you before it happens, so that when it happens, you may believe.* Trap sprung!

What good would it be if Jesus were talking about a far future (after we're dead) event in verses 2 and 3, and then says that He is helping our belief (after we're dead) when that future event happens (after we're dead)? Will our belief need help then, after we're dead? The answer is obvious, because belief is for this life, while we live in the flesh.

So, we have a misunderstanding of Jesus' words based on the word mansions and on the non-New Testament (even, I would say, non-Biblical) idea of heaven being God's house. Now that the mansions and other nice houses have been removed, where does that leave us? Didn't Jesus say that He was going away to prepare a place for us? Again, the idea that Jesus went away to heaven to build nice houses for us does not fit the context of the chapter, and it has nothing to do with God's revelation in the New Testament.

He also said, "if it were not so, I would have told you". This phrase bothered me for longer than I can recall. It is like Jesus was saying, "If there were not going to be mansions, I would have told you that you were not getting mansions." Even though I do not understand at God's level, I could not make sense of that logic.

There is, however, a precedent for what I think Jesus was saying. In John 12:24 He said, *Truly, truly, I say to you, unless a grain of wheat falls into the earth and dies, it remains alone; but if it dies, it bears much fruit.* Jesus said that one grain, Himself, will produce many other identical grains. He was the one unique grain on the earth at the time. Likewise, when He spoke those words in John 14, He was the one unique tabernacle of God on the earth (John 1:14). Through His death and resurrection many more tabernacles of God (us!) would be produced. He would not remain forever as God's only habitation. **This** is what He would have told us! If it were not true that we would also become dwelling places of God in the Spirit (Ephesians 2:22), He would have told us! If He were to remain as the singular tabernacle of God, He would have told us. Just as we are to become the many grains from one grain, we also become God's many dwelling places produced by the death and resurrection of the one Tabernacle.

The unique One becoming many seems to be a New Testament principal: one grain becoming many (John 12:24); the only begotten Son becoming the firstborn among many brethren (Romans 8:29); one body broken becoming one body with many members (1 Corinthians 12:12,27); one river of life becoming many rivers of living water (John 4:10,14 and 7:38); the one tabernacle of God becoming many (John 14:2) and incorporating many (1 Corinthians 3:17b, Ephesians 2:21-22, etc.).

Jesus also told us where He was going and where He wants to bring us. Verse 14:6: *no one comes **to the Father**....* Does coming to the Father have to mean a change in location, i.e. heaven? I do not think so, of course.

The Lord's response in verse 6 came after this exchange in verses 3 to 5. *"If I go and prepare a place for you, I will come again and receive you to Myself, that where I am, there you may be also. And you know the way where I am going." Thomas said to Him, "Lord, we do not know where You are going, how do we know the way?" Jesus said to him, "I am the way, and the truth, and the life; no one comes to the Father but through Me."*

When is it that Jesus would come again and receive us to Himself? Maybe He already has!

We have looked at verses 28 and 29 already, but let us review. *You heard that **I said to you**, "I go away, and I will come to you."* When did Jesus say that? Again, this was verse 3. Referring to that previous statement, He said, *Now I have told you **before** it happens, so that **when it happens**, you may believe.* Helping our belief is related to this age, when faith is required. I mention going and coming again to help **your** belief, to help **you** to understand the divine revelation as it was intended.

How could we hope to live the Christian life if the Lord's going and returning have not already transpired? Why should James and Peter have to wait 2000 years for the first resurrection in order to be received by the Lord or received to Him? The answer is that they did have to wait a couple days, until after the Lord's resurrection, which is also mentioned in John 14.

What about the last part of verse 6, the part about Jesus being the only way to heaven? Oh, wait. It doesn't say that, does it? But I have heard preachers on radio and television and others rephrase the verse in that way. Probably you have been taught to understand it in that way. Why do we not understand that Jesus is talking about the present? No need to wait! Through Him I **have** come to the Father! Do we need more evidence? Have a look at Ephesians 2:18. *For through Him we both* (Jews and gentiles) *have our access in one Spirit **to the Father**.* This is practically the same verse as John 14:6! John 14:6 says "through Me," and Ephesians 2:18 says "through Him" and "in one Spirit." Both say "to the Father"! Do you think that Ephesians 2 is for the bye-and-bye? Let me be bold and assume that you do not. And I say that neither is John 14 for some later time.

Jesus said that He is "the way, the truth, and the life." He is my way right now. He is my truth today. He is my life. In Him I have access **right now** to my Father. I have come to my Father, and He has come to me. No waiting!

Consider this. At the end of chapter 13 Jesus had just told Peter that he would deny Him. Then the Lord's next words were, "Do not let your heart be troubled." I ask you, which would bring comfort to Peter's heart: that he would have a nice house after he dies, or that the triune God will make His home in Peter's heart? For me the answer is easy, and I hope you are being persuaded of the same.

Now I will show you that the rest of chapter 14 is Jesus' explanation of **how** He planned to come to us and how this relates to our being the abodes of our Father's house.

First, Jesus showed us His relationship to the Father in verses 7 and 9-11. Verse 7 says, *If you had known Me, you would have known My Father also; from now on you know Him, and have seen Him.* Verse 9 says, *He who has seen Me has seen the Father.* In both verses 10 and 11 He declared, *I am in the Father, and the Father is in Me.*

After explaining His relationship with the Father, Jesus began to show His relationship to the Spirit in verse 16, calling Him another Helper, but also saying in verse 17, *but you **know** Him because He abides **with** you and **will** be in you.*

Notice the tense of Jesus' verbs in the last two paragraphs. Regarding the Father, He says, *from now on* (starting now) *you know Him* (present tense) *and have seen Him* (present perfect). Who had they spent the previous three and a half years with? Who have the disciples known all this time? Jesus, of course! Who have they seen? Also Jesus! Regarding the Spirit, He told the eleven (Judas had left) that they already know Him, because He was already abiding with them. Again, who do they know? The answer is Jesus! Furthermore, the One who was already abiding **with** them, whom they already knew, would be **in** them!

In this Jesus told His disciples **how** He was coming to them as He had promised in verse 3. He would be coming to them as the Spirit. Then later He said (verse 18), *I will not leave you as orphans; I will come to you*. Finally, He explained how it is that we are in the Father in verse 20: *In that day you will know that I am in My Father, and you in Me, and I in you*. In which day? A day far off into the future? No! In the day that He, as the Spirit and with the Father, came into us, we were able to know that we are in Christ and in the Father! For the disciples this was on the day of Christ's resurrection. Chapter 20 of John covers this. Verse 20:22 reveals that Jesus breathed upon them and said, *Receive the Holy Spirit*. The disciples were, and we are, in the Father, and verse 14:6 is realized!

Lastly, we come to verse 14:23, the verse where we see the second usage of this word for abode. *Jesus answered and said to him, "If anyone loves Me, he will keep My word; and My Father will love him, and We will come to him and make Our abode with him*. Once again, this promise is for our life in this age. The many abodes in verse 2 are the same abodes that God indwells in verse 23. This is the church!

Returning to the earlier point, I hope that you can now see that this is what Jesus meant when He said, *If it were not so, I would have told you*. If He was going to be the Father's only tabernacle, or abode, then Jesus would have told us that. The first chapter of John's gospel tells us, *And the Word became flesh and dwelt* (tabernacled) *among us, and we saw His glory, glory as of the only begotten from the Father, full of grace and truth* (John 1:14).

While at first Jesus was the Father's only begotten, the goal was (Romans 8:29) to become the firstborn among many brothers! So now, which makes more sense: "I would have told you if you weren't getting mansions," or "I would have told you if the Father did not intend to make His abode in you?" After having just told

Peter that he was going to betray his Lord (verse 13:38), which makes more sense: "That's okay, you will get a nice big house after you die," or "God wants to make His home in your heart"? Which better fits the revelation of the New Testament? Which fits the context of the rest of chapter 14? Which fits the context of verse 14:29?

I hope you can see now that the entirety of chapter 14 of John's gospel has to do with our relationship in Christ to the triune God. To apply the first six verses to future events dismisses the context of the chapter, including verse 29. Four times in this chapter Jesus said that He (or "We") would come to us. Do we get to pick and choose whether He meant a future event in the first case (verse 3) and a present day event in the others?

The other times that Jesus said He is coming to us are verses 18, 23, and 28. Verse 18: *I will not leave you as orphans; I will come to you.* Here is the last part of verse 23. *...My Father will love him, and We will come to him and make Our abode with him.* I think we have no trouble understanding that verses 18 and 23 are relevant to our current existence, so why not the first mention in verse 3? I hope that I have convinced you that verse 3 is for this present life.

I have mentioned verses 28 and 29, but beginning with verse 27 Jesus summarized the beginning of the chapter. *Do not let your heart be troubled, nor let it be fearful.* I am going away. I am going to the Father. I will return to you. This ties the beginning to the end, and Jesus told the disciples so that they would believe after it all happens.

One more time… Verse 29 says, *Now I have told you before it happens, so that **when** it happens, you may believe.* Jesus told the disciples that He was going away and coming back, so that they would believe when it happened. What good would that do if Jesus had been referring to His second coming? Jesus wants us to believe now! Therefore, all four mentions of His coming in chapter fourteen have to be for the present age!

The reality of this became known to the eleven after Christ's resurrection. Again, John 20:22 says, *He breathed on them and said* to them, *"Receive the Holy Spirit."* This was the fulfillment of John 14 in their lives, as it also is fulfilled in ours.

Remember that when Mary Magdalene saw the Lord, He told her not to touch Him because He had not yet ascended to the Father (John 20:17). (NASB phrased it as "**stop** clinging," but every other translation that I checked said something like "do not...") Maybe He was going somewhere? *Stop clinging to Me, for I have not yet ascended to the Father.* Verse 17 continues, the Lord saying, *But go to My brethren and say to them, "I ascend to My Father and your Father, and My God and your God."* He has just told Mary that He was going, as He said in John 14:3, and, more specifically, that He was going to the Father, as He said in 14:28. When did He return? Later that same day (verse 20:19)! And we know that He had gone to the Father by this time, because He leisurely spent time with the disciples, He allowed them to touch Him, and because He dispensed the Holy Spirit into them, completely in accord with what He said would happen in chapter 14!

This brings me back to the issue that I mentioned at the beginning of this chapter: Was John 20:22 a symbolic act? Jesus **said** (to Mary) that He was ascending to the Father, and He said (to the disciples) "**receive** the Holy Spirit." These two things happened! The Son of Man accomplished all that the Father had determined. I have explained above what John 14 is about. Jesus was going away and coming back. His going was to the Father, so if He went away and came back to them (which He obviously did), then by His own definition, He had to have gone to the Father after meeting with Mary!

And look at all the believing! Luke 24:41 mentions "their joy and amazement," and John 20:20 says that "the disciples then rejoiced when they saw the Lord." They did not believe the reports of those who had seen the resurrected Jesus. Mark 16:14 says, *He reproached them for their unbelief and hardness of heart, because they had not believed those who had seen Him after He had risen.* But when He personally came to them, well, **then** the believing happened! John 14 fulfilled.

To summarize, chapter 14 is framed by verses 1-3 and verses 27-29. In verses 1-3 Jesus told the disciples to not be afraid and what He was going to do. Verse 27 reminds them to not be afraid, and verses 28 and 29 reminded them that He **did** tell them what He was going to do, and everything in between is the divine explanation, in various aspects and in heavenly detail, **how** the wonderful triune God makes His home in our hearts!

Context is extremely important to understanding the Bible. I have presented: 1) local context within chapter 14 itself, including verse 29; 2) context within John's gospel; 3) the context of God's New Testament economy; and 4) the context of the whole revelation of God's Word (heaven is not God's home). To say that verses 2 and 3 refer to mansions or rooms relies on extremely narrow context, which I would say is based on preconditioned thinking. I know that is harsh, but how does one discard all the scriptures and context that has been presented here? How can verse 29 be discarded? This seems to be one of the most ignored verses in the Bible.

There is no mention of the bride in this chapter, but to me John 14 is the heart of the Bible. Nowhere else in God's Word is His one-threeness unveiled like it is here. No where else is His process explained so concisely by which He makes His home in our hearts. It is all here in John 14. The bride is not mentioned, but this is how she is produced.

God's wisdom knows no bounds. There are many threads that course through the Bible, but they all will come together at the grand conclusion of His wonderous plan. We also see that when He spoke, whether directly or through His chosen vessels, He often spoke to more than one audience. This was especially evident in prophecies about the Lord's birth and His life in the flesh, in which a word was directed to a person or situation in the Old Testament that also contained an element of something about Jesus.

During His earthly ministry, Jesus sometimes spoke of the then present or near future while also including words concerning things farther down the road. I believe this is exhibited in Matthew 24 when the Lord spoke of the coming destruction of Jerusalem and also about events that will transpire at the end of this age.

Here in John 14 and the other gospels there is also something else going on, something even deeper and of more significance than the Lord's last supper and all the wonderful spiritual details that we see in that. This other thing has much to do with the subject of this book. It is the betrothal of the Groom to His bride. This is the heart of the Bible.

Betrothal

Weddings are a big deal. So are the preparations. In the centuries before and after that first century A.D. the Galilean and Jewish weddings were every bit a big deal. What, you didn't know about the Galilean wedding? Neither had I. In a Bible study in the spring of 2022 a knowledgeable brother mentioned the Galilean wedding when we were on the topic of the Lord's last supper in Matthew's gospel. At the time I was considering what and how I should write about the new Jerusalem, so his comment caught my attention. I talked to him after the meeting in the parking lot. "Are you saying that the Galilean wedding is different from the Jewish wedding?" I do not remember his exact words, but you can guess the answer.

That brother's name was Steve Reiser. He went to the Lord later that year. I had not started working on the book yet, so I did not follow up with him. That left me to search out others on the web, and I found quite a few brothers who have spoken or written about the Galilean wedding. They will be listed at the end of this chapter.

What strikes me deeply about this is how the Lord brought two brothers into the same fellowship from different parts of this country, at different times, and then one of them "randomly" said something that the other needed to hear. All of us in this Bible study appreciated Steve over the years, so I will not suggest that this one event was the only reason that Steve was among us; but things like this stand apart in one's experience.

Jesus came out of Galilee, and that is where He found His disciples, with the possible exception of Judas Iscariot. In the three and a half years that He spent teaching them, He used many illustrations that were familiar to them, especially the wedding.

Why the wedding? I hope that after reading the previous chapters, you have an appreciation. What God is doing is rather complicated. Some of the things that Jesus dealt with are our sins, our sin nature, our redemption, our sanctification, and His enemy satan. There are other matters as well, as well as more details relative to those listed. When it comes to us, we are His church, His body, God's temple, His ambassadors, the light of the world. We are many things to Him, as He is to us. Besides all these, Jesus is the bridegroom, and we are His bride.

It is for that last reason (bridegroom and bride) that I wrote this book. I hope we can see the vision of the bride and better understand the importance of this marriage in God's eternal plan.

I hope I do not bore you as I go through the process. As you read, try to recall events and details that you have read in the Bible.

The Parents

The betrothal in those days began with the parents, usually the father of a son. That father might see a girl that he thinks will be a very good wife for his son. Maybe he is aware that her parents are good citizens. One day he invites the girl's father, with his family, to come for a feast. After some wining and dining, maybe for two days, the boy's father makes a marriage proposal to the girl's father. Love has nothing to do with it, and the children might be quite young, maybe not even 10 years old. If the idea seems good to the girl's father, the two of them get down to business.

What business? They negotiate the bride price. They negotiate the groom's dowry. The children have no say in the matter. When the fathers come to an agreement, all the details of the *ketubah* are written in duplicate. The *ketubah* is the marriage contract, a covenant, and each father gets a copy, which they keep until the betrothal. That's right, we have not gotten to the betrothal yet!

Note: I found more than one way to spell some of the Jewish words used here. Please be generous if you think I am making an error.

The bride price is paid by the groom's father. It is heavily negotiated between the two fathers, and it can be quite a sum, depending on the families' status. There could be camels, sheep, goats, and money involved.

When the children get older, yet still only 14 or 15 years old, the betrothal ceremony can take place. This takes place at a city gate, where transactions would take place that need witnesses. It was at a city gate where Boaz offered the close relative of Naomi the opportunity to purchase her field (Ruth 4:1).

The Betrothal

At the city gate a *hoopah,* a canopy, is set up. The groom, the bride, the parents, friends, and the witnesses (who just happen to be there) are all gathered. The *ketubah,* which was previously agreed to, is read for all to hear. The groom's father presents the bride price to the bride's father, who inspects it and receives it.

The groom pays a dowry to the bride (or to her father) as a down payment of sorts. He forfeits the dowry if he does not go through with the wedding, whether it be for reasons within his control (divorce) or not, including his death.

Gifts are exchanged between the groom and bride. The groom usually gives a ring, but if he is poor, he might give a small coin to the bride. The bride usually gives a flask of ointment to the groom.

After all of the exchanges of payments and gifts, hopefully everything is going smoothly. At this point the groom will offer his bride the cup of joy. This is undiluted wine. This is where the Galilean betrothal has its greatest departure from the Jewish betrothal: the Galilean bride can decide not to marry the groom! In that case she will decline the cup. If the bride is willing to marry the groom, she will drink from the cup and return it to the groom. He will drink from it also, and then he will say so that all the witnesses can hear, "You are now covenanted to me by the laws of Moses, and I will not drink of this cup again until I drink it anew with you in my father's house."

The young teenagers are now married...legally and morally. Nevertheless, they will not live together for about another year. There is a lot to do! The groom returns to his father's house and will spend most of his time getting ready for the next big day. He needs to build a habitation for himself and his bride; he needs to procure enough food for a feast that will last seven days; and he needs to prepare white garments for all of the wedding guests. The bride has her duties, mainly preparing wedding garments for herself and her bridesmaids. During this time the two will not see each other except for occasional glimpses, but the groom and the bride will send gifts to each other. Whenever the bride goes outside her home, she will wear a veil, being considered as consecrated, bought for a price.

The Wedding

The anticipation builds as that year (it could be longer) begins to come around. The son puts the finishing touches on his new abode and is eager to hear his father's declaration that it is ready. The bride and her maids sleep together in her home. They even sleep in their wedding garments so that they will be ready at a moment's notice. They also need to keep their lamps trimmed and have enough extra oil in vessels. The streets are very dark at night, and that is usually when the groom arrives.

One day the groom's father evaluates his son's new abode and decides that it is ready. That night the father wakes his son and says, "Son, go get your bride." What a night this will be! He gets his friends, and they all head to his bride's home. They do not take a direct route, and this is not a quiet procession. No! They make as much noise as they can! The bride and her friends are awakened, but not only them; all who live along the route are brought out of their sleep. I used to think how inconsiderate that is, but after studying this process, I found out that many of those wakened are the wedding guests. They also need to quickly make their way to the wedding feast. The indirect route helps to make sure that they are awakened.

The groom and his friends move toward the bride's home in a meandering procession. Because the bride and her maids are sleeping in their wedding garments, they need a little time to smooth out the wrinkles and fix their hair. The slow procession gives them this time. The bride also puts on a veil. The groom blows a *shofar* (ram's horn) to announce his progress. As the groom and his friends draw near, the bride and her maids go out to meet them. The bride is seated in a chair that is resting on two horizontal poles. The chair is lifted on the poles, and the bride is carried to the groom's house. This is called flying the bride to the father's house.

Meanwhile, the wedding guests are making their way to the feast. When they arrive, white garments are given to them to wear for the duration. They have to be on time, because once the door is shut, no one will be allowed in.

Out on the streets the procession quickly makes its way to the father's home. This is a direct route, not the wandering method used when getting the bride. Upon arrival the groom's father shuts the door, and the groom and the still-veiled bride spend a little time with the guests, but it is not long. They do few customary things, including taking one more sip from the cup of joy.

They enter into the room that the groom had prepared, and the marriage is soon consummated. And that is to say, soon. The best man, the groom's friend, is standing outside the room. What?! He is waiting for word from the groom that the couple have done the deed. The best man then announces this to those in the wedding feast, which causes much rejoicing and celebration!

The newlyweds remain in isolation for seven days, almost the entire duration of the wedding feast. After the seven days, the groom and his **unveiled** bride rejoin the feast. Now everyone can see the beauty of the bride!

I told the story of how I came to know that the Galilean wedding was distinct from the Jewish wedding. I went to many sources. It was not easy to sort through everything, and there was not 100% agreement about several details. What I present in this chapter is my best understanding. A few sources wrote of the Jewish wedding, seeming to not consider the Galilean, [perhaps conflating the two. For example, s]ome sources say that the wedding date in the Jewish tradition was predetermined and known by all, following other regional customs, but other sources describe the date as undetermined.

[Below,] in no particular order, are the sources I used. I want to give attribution, of course, but this will give you a start if you want to look into the wedding customs for yourself.

Jay McCarl   https://jaymccarl.com/
A Galilean Wedding   https://youtu.be/xjuzK1fwDLQ
Broken Bread – An Ancient Look at the First Last Supper   2009   Biblical Dinners Publishing

A Carpenter's View   It is key: He was a Galilean. So were His disciples.   March 11, 2020
https://teachingforsotzambia.com/2020/03/11/it-is-key-he-was-a-galilean-so-were-his-disciples/

Nathan Boehm   The Galilean Wedding   Aug 8, 2022
https://www.richmondfwc.com/post/the-galilean-wedding

Bill Alderson   A Galilean Wedding   Mar 3, 2021
https://ggwo.org/a-galilean-wedding/

Julie Saunders   Ancient Galilean Wedding & Bride of Christ!   Pray 4 Zion   Alf & July 1, 2021
https://www.pray4zion.org/AncientGalileanWeddingBrideofChrist.html

Robert Wimer   A Galilean Wedding   June 12, 2022
https://robertwimer.com/a-galilean-wedding/

Zola Lovitt   A Christian Love Story   1978   Mass Market Paperback

Olive Branch Fellowship
https://theolivebranchfellowship.com/teachings

The Bride in the Old Testament

Some might be surprised to realize that God made a marriage covenant with Israel after he led them out of Egypt. Everything that transpired at Mount Sinai is a microcosm of Israel's history. Jeremiah explained it in one sentence (Jeremiah 31:31-32). *"Behold, days are coming," declares the LORD, "when I will make a new covenant with the house of Israel and with the house of Judah, not like **the covenant which I made** with their fathers in the day I took them by the hand to bring them out of the land of Egypt, My covenant which they broke, **although I was a husband to them**," declares the LORD.*

Jehovah Himself (imagine that!) declared that He was a husband to Israel, but Israel broke the marriage covenant, the *ketubah*. What happened? How do we go on from here?

Please refer to chapter 5, The Betrothal, while reading this. I cannot make everything fit chronologically, but the main theme seems to hold water. Let us retrace the story.

The Ketubah

In Exodus we have two fathers (a Father and a father). The Son's Father invited Moses, the other father, up to the mountain in Exodus 19:3. There are instructions and warnings from God in the rest of the chapter, and then in chapter 20 we have the *ketubah*, yes, the ten commandments. Two copies are made, one for the Father and one for the father. The two tablets were not the way they are typically portrayed, with five commands on each tablet. According to the way covenants were made, there would have been two identical copies. Both tablets contained the complete *ketubah*, identical copies.

The *ketubah* did not consist of only the big ten, but many other instructions that are found in chapters 20-23. Verse 24:4a says, *Moses wrote down all the words of the LORD,* but verse 24:12 says that God **also** wrote the same. *Now the LORD said to Moses, "Come up to Me on the mountain and remain there, and I will give you the* *stone tablets with the law **and** the commandment which **I have written** for their instruction."* We see by this that two copies were made (Moses' copy and the copy that God wrote), and each copy contained the entirety of God's speaking in these chapters of Exodus.

The next seven chapters are instructions for the tabernacle, and chapter 31 ends (verse 18) with, *When He had finished speaking with him upon Mount Sinai, He gave Moses the two tablets of the testimony, tablets of stone, written by the finger of God.* Exodus 32:15 says that they were written on both sides. Why all this writing? This was the *ketubah*! These were the conditions of the betrothal.

Well, this seems quite one-sided. These tablets contained all of the bride's obligations. In Exodus 23, from verse 20 to the end, God explains in general terms how Israel will take the land that He would give to them (verses 20, 23, and 27-31), but interspersed are warnings that Israel should have nothing to do with the people that are being driven out and especially nothing to do with their gods. What about the Husband? This does not seem very *ketubah*-like on His part. What are God's obligations? Dare we ask?

Genesis 15

The basis of Israel's taking the land is found in Genesis 15. The Husband's part of the *ketubah* can be seen in Genesis 15. "But that was more than 430 years before the Exodus!" I think you will see something very marvelous and inspiring. God's Word is a masterpiece.

Genesis 15:4-5: *Then behold, the word of the LORD came to him, saying, "This man will not be your heir* (referring to the servant Eliezer); *but one who will come forth from your own body, he shall be your heir." And He took him outside and said, "Now look toward the heavens, and count the stars, if you are able to count them." And He said to him, "So shall your descendants be."* Verse 6 tells us that Abram believed God and that his believing was accounted to Abram as righteousness.

But that was not the end of the conversation. God continues (verse 7), *And He said to him, "I am the LORD who brought you out of Ur of the Chaldeans, to give you this land to possess it."* Abram's response? Verse 8: *He said, "O Lord GOD, how may I know that I will possess it?"* Huh? After being counted as righteous for believing, Abram now questions God? Interestingly, rather than scold Abram, God initiated a legally binding procedure that was the practice in those days. Another reference to this practice is in Jeremiah 34:18.

God had Abram kill a heifer, a goat, and a ram, and cut the carcasses in half. He laid the halves in two rows, with a space between the rows for two people to walk between. Abram also killed a turtledove and a pigeon, but he did not cut them in half. He laid one bird in each row. The two parties would walk between the two rows. They would recite their promises and state that if one failed to keep his promise, then he would justifiably end up like the carcasses. This was a very serious matter.

When the day ended, God put Abram to sleep. Abram did not walk between the rows. God walked it by Himself. Here are verses 17 and 18. *It came about when the sun had set, that it was very dark, and behold, there appeared a smoking oven and a flaming torch which passed between these pieces. On that day the LORD made a* **covenant** *with Abram, saying, "To your descendants I have given this land, From the river of Egypt as far as the great river, the river Euphrates.*

I understand if you have trouble seeing this as part of a marriage contract. It seems more like a land contract. I pray that it becomes clearer as this chapter continues.

The Harlot

It is not difficult to find references to Israel being a harlot. I think the first mention is in Judges 2:17. *Yet they did not listen to their judges, for they played the harlot after other gods and bowed themselves down to them.* But the first time that it happened was right there at Mount Sinai.

Chapter 31 of Exodus ends with God giving to Moses "the two tablets of the testimony," two copies of the contract. The Hebrew word also means "witness,", and that is what a contract is…a witness. Two copies provide two witnesses.

At the bottom of the mountain the people grew impatient with Moses' long absence and said to Aaron (verse 32:1), *Come, make us a god who will go before us; as for this Moses, the man who brought us up from the land of Egypt, we do not know what has become of him.* Everyone knows that Aaron made the gold calf. What many might overlook is that they thought they were doing this in order to worship God. Verse 32:5 says, *Now when Aaron saw this, he built an altar before it; and Aaron made a proclamation and said, "Tomorrow shall be a feast to the LORD."* "Lord" here is the name Jehovah. No matter how they might justify it, this calf was an idol, and Aaron built an altar for it. The next day people brought burnt offerings and peace offerings, *and the people sat down to eat and to drink, and rose up to play* (verse 6b). That last phrase refers to something akin to orgies, which was a significant aspect of the idol worship that was to come later.

In Moses' rational appeal to God to not destroy the people (verse 32:13), he included God's promise to Abram in Genesis 15. *"Remember Abraham, Isaac, and Israel, Your servants to whom You swore by Yourself, and said to them, 'I will multiply your descendants as the stars of the heavens, and all this land of which I have spoken I will give to your descendants, and they shall inherit it forever.'"*

And so it began. The betrothed bride was called a harlot over three dozen times in the prophetical books. What's a Husband to do? God called Israel and Judah to repentance over and over. Once in a while Judah would return to their God because of a faithful king, but even then, the high places (for idol worship) were not removed, except in the case of Hezekiah. Hezekiah removed the high places, but his son Manasseh rebuilt them. The northern kingdom, Israel, never did have a good king.

Remember that the groom and the bride are married when their betrothal takes place. They are husband and wife; but they do not live together. The marriage is not yet consummated, but they are married. This is why Joseph considered whether to secretly give Mary a certificate of divorce when she was pregnant with Jesus. Keep this in mind as we consider Israel's relationship to God in the Old Testament.

Divorce!

This marriage was not working out. Making it even more complicated, the one nation was now two. Through the prophet Hosea, God showed how He would deal with the northern kingdom, Israel. An overview is in the first three chapters of Hosea. God told Hosea to marry a harlot. In chapter two, verse 2a, God says, *Contend with your mother, contend, for she is not my wife, and I am not her husband.* Does that sound like a divorce? Look at Jeremiah 3:8. *And I saw that for all the adulteries of faithless Israel, I had sent her away and given her a writ of divorce.* Wow.

What about Judah? In divorcing Israel, did God divorce Judah at the same time? Did He divorce Judah separately? More likely, Judah, "her treacherous sister," was not divorced by God. I cannot say that for sure, but we can read some harsh words for her. I quoted the first half of Jeremiah 3:8 concerning Israel. Here is the rest of that verse. *...yet her treacherous sister Judah did not fear; but she went and was a harlot also.* And verse 10: *"Yet in spite of all this her treacherous sister Judah did not return to Me with all her heart, but rather in deception," declares the LORD.*

Eventually God left Judah to her idolatry. Chapters nine and ten of Ezekiel demonstrate this. In chapter eight Ezekiel saw all the great abominations taking place inside God's temple. Then in verse 9:3 we see God moving from the cherub in the Holy of Holies. I do not know why "cherub" here is singular. I checked various commentaries to find out if anyone addressed that. I did not find anyone who did. Nevertheless, there is total agreement that this first move of "the glory of God" is a move out of the Holiest Place. From that location the Glory moved to the threshold of the temple. Verse 10:4 mentions that initial move and adds, *and the temple was filled with the cloud and the court was filled with the brightness of the glory of the LORD.* God's glory is now outside the temple. The next move was above cherubim who were in the air (verse 10:18), and above the east gate of the house (verse 10:19). The last move is given in verse 11:23. *The glory of the LORD went up from the midst of the city and stood over the mountain which is east of the city.* That mountain is the Mount of Olives.

Judah and Israel had clearly violated the terms of the *ketubah*. I mentioned the high places that were a constant thorn in the side of God's people, but what Ezekiel saw in chapter 8 was taking place inside God's house! No wonder God left.

Hope!

God's plan will never be thwarted. Even though Israel and Judah were not faithful to their Betrothed, He will regain the hearts of His people. Returning to Hosea, we see in verse 2:14 that *Therefore, behold, I will allure her, bring her into the wilderness and speak kindly to her.* The result is in verse 16: *"It will come about in that day,"* declares the LORD, *"That you will call Me Ishi and will no longer call Me Baali."* "Baali" means "my master." "Ishi" means "my husband." *You will call Me Ishi.* What a loving Husband!

This renewed relationship is also given to us in Isaiah 54:5-8. Here are selections from that passage.

> Verse 5a – *For your husband is your Maker*
> Verse 6a – *For the Lord has called you, like a wife forsaken and grieved in spirit*
> Verse 7 – *For a brief moment I forsook you, but with great compassion I will gather you*
> Verse 8 – *In an outburst of anger I hid My face from you for a moment, but with everlasting lovingkindness I will have compassion on you," says the LORD your Redeemer.*

Even though Hosea 2:14 makes it seem like a pleasant transition, many other passages reveal an arduous process, including the first

13 verses of Hosea 2. Verse 13 summarizes: *"I will punish her for the days of the Baals when she used to offer sacrifices to them and adorn herself with her earrings and jewelry, and follow her lovers, so that she forgot Me," declares the LORD.*

Judah returned from Babylon after 70 years of captivity but found themselves under one repressive regime after another. Nevertheless, after returning from Babylon, they were determined to follow the law like they never had before, even to the point of adding their own laws, which became known as their tradition. You can say that they loved their law so much, that when their Betrothed came on the scene, they did not recognize Him. They actually had their Husband crucified!

Is this section not titled "Hope!"? We know that there is hope! The prophets declared hope. We know that there is a promised future that is certain, full of glory, purpose, and God's presence.

But a major problem stands in the way.

The Covenants

That *ketubah* became a problem. From the beginning the bride did not maintain her contractual obligations, and when she finally decided to try to keep it, she overreacted by adding to it.

The prophets wrote about a new covenant, and Jesus spoke of it at the Last Supper. But how can we get from here to there? The *ketubah* is legally binding, on both the groom and the bride. Not even God can merely toss it aside, wipe His hands a few times, and say, "Well, let's try another way."

There is a legal way to get out of the first *ketubah*, "weak as it was through the flesh," but it would necessarily be very demanding. Paul told us how in Romans 7:2. *For the married woman is bound by law to her husband while he is living; but if her husband dies, she is released from the law concerning the husband.* The middle of verse 7:3 continues, *if her husband dies, she is free from the law*, or the *ketubah* in our discussion.

You saw this coming, did you not? But this is a new perspective. Not only did the Husband die, the bride also died! Staying in Romans, verse 7:4a says, *Therefore, my brethren, you also were made to die to the Law through the body of Christ.* In this Paul is including Gentiles. The first covenant was made with Israel, but in order to enlarge the bride, Gentiles are now included. But in fact, Gentiles were included from the beginning. Paul made this case in his letter to the churches in Galatia. Verse 3:7 says, *Therefore, be sure that it is those who are of faith who are sons of Abraham.* And verse 3:13 says that Christ became a curse for us by hanging on a tree, *in order that in Christ Jesus the blessing of Abraham might come to the Gentiles, so that we would receive the promise of the Spirit through faith* (verse 14). Thank the Lord for that!

We are all dead, both the groom and the bride. We are released from the first *ketubah*, but only through death. Covenants are between living persons. You know what's coming.

The first part of Romans 7:4 is quoted above. Here is the complete verse. *Therefore, my brethren, you also were made to die to the Law through the body of Christ, so that you might be joined* *to another, **to Him who was raised from the dead**, in order that we might bear fruit for God.* The Groom is now alive! More than that, we also are alive. Ephesians 2:5a refers to the bride. *Even when we were dead in our transgressions, made us alive together with Christ.* We are alive! In Christ's death, we died. In Christ's resurrection, we live!

A significant part of Paul's writings deals with the termination of the old covenant and the inauguration of the new. We think of law versus grace, and certainly Paul paints that scenario, but the real story is about two marriage covenants, two contracts. The first was ineffective because the bride did not fulfill her obligations, to the extent of being unfaithful to her Husband. But a contract is a contract, and only death can terminate it. This is what Paul explained in Romans 7.

The writer of Hebrews also explained it quite clearly in chapter 8. Verses 8 and 9:

For finding fault with them, He says,
"BEHOLD, DAYS ARE COMING, SAYS THE LORD,
WHEN I WILL EFFECT A NEW COVENANT
WITH THE HOUSE OF ISRAEL AND WITH THE HOUSE OF JUDAH;
NOT LIKE THE COVENANT WHICH I MADE WITH THEIR FATHERS
ON THE DAY WHEN I TOOK THEM BY THE HAND
TO LEAD THEM OUT OF THE LAND OF EGYPT;
FOR THEY DID NOT CONTINUE IN MY COVENANT,
AND I DID NOT CARE FOR THEM, SAYS THE LORD.

Verse 13a concludes, *When He said, "A new covenant," He has made the first obsolete.*

A lot happened on that cross. Yes, Jesus died for our sins and redeemed us from the curse, but there was so much more that Jesus did there. One of those things was terminating all parties of the first covenant. Some want to argue that we still need to keep the law. But we died! The first contract is null and void. There is no obligation to that contract. I hope you can see how freeing that is! As Paul states in Romans 8:2, we are *free from the law of sin and of death*!

Jesus still wants a bride, but two things are needed: people who are living, and a new covenant, a new *ketubah*. I am being repetitious, but Matthew, Mark, and Luke show the establishment of the new contract at the last supper, and Romans 7:4 and Ephesians 2:5 show that all parties have been raised up in resurrection. What a magnificent plan!

There remains a question, though. What are the terms of the new *ketubah*? Recall Jeremiah 31:31. *"Behold, days are coming," declares the LORD, "when I will make a new covenant with the house of Israel and with the house of Judah."* Ah, a new *ketubah*! We can know that this is a new *ketubah* because it is compared directly to the first covenant, which is identified as the first *ketubah* in verse 32: *"not like the covenant which I made with their fathers in the day I took them by the hand to bring them out of the land of Egypt, My covenant which they broke, although I was a husband to them," declares the LORD.*

Verse 31:33 then gives us the terms of the contract. *"But this is the covenant which I will make with the house of Israel after those days," declares the LORD, "I will put My law within them and on their heart I will write it; and I will be their God, and they shall be My people.* That's it? That's it! A lot is implied in "it," but **this** law now will be *the law of the Spirit of life in Christ Jesus*, which has set us free *from the law of sin and of death* (Romans 8:2). James called this law the "law of liberty" (James 1:25).

We are not lawless. I have been called lawless by some (on social media, not knowing anything about me) who insist that we need to keep the old law. But the law of the Spirit of life is much stricter and higher than the old law. Chapters 5, 6, and 7 in Matthew are proof of that. Even though I still do things contrary to the law of life, this living law is being written on my heart. It is becoming part of me! My nature is being changed! Ezekiel 36:26-27 tell us this. *Moreover, I will give you a new heart and put a new spirit within you; and I will remove the heart of stone from your flesh and give you a heart of flesh. I will put My Spirit within you and cause you to walk in My statutes, and you will be careful to observe My ordinances.*

"But aren't these verses talking about Israel?" Yes, but Israel will receive later that which we are currently receiving from our triune God. The divine life, which we have received by believing in Jesus, and which we continually receive by allowing the Spirit to write the divine life into us, will be given to Israel when they also believe!

There remains a new question. What about Genesis 15? If the old *ketubah* is obsolete, what happened to the first covenant that God made with Abram? Is it also void? Let us see what Paul said. *What I am saying is this: the Law, which came four hundred and thirty years later, does not invalidate a covenant previously ratified by God, so as to nullify the promise* (Galatians 3:17). Genesis 15:18 says that God made a covenant with Abram, but Abram did not walk through the carcasses. God walked it alone. This covenant stands, even through Israel's unfaithfulness, even through divorce, and even through the deaths of the two parties.

The restored nation of Israel will reside in the land designated by God. The **spiritual** descendants will inherit the world. *For the promise to Abraham or to his descendants that he would be heir of the world was not through the Law, but through the righteousness of faith* (Romans 4:13). *For this reason it is by faith, in order that it may be in accordance with grace, so that the promise will be guaranteed to all the descendants, not only to those who are of the Law, but also to those who are of the faith of Abraham, who is the father of us all* (Romans 4:16). God is so thorough!

I hope that this short discussion of the two covenants was helpful. It should add another dimension to explanations in the various epistles. It should also provide new depth of understanding to the new covenant unveiled by the Lord at His last supper.

God did not give up on a bride for His Son. He chose a people, and He was a husband to them. But the wife was unfaithful and did not return His love. A divorce did not nullify the marriage contract;

only death could do that. The Father's marvelous plan resulted in death of both through the all-inclusive death of His Son. Now the way is clear for a new *ketubah*.

This new covenant is so-o-o much better! The bride will be (and is) much happier! Thank you, Father, for allowing us to be a part of this. We worship You for Your marvelous plan. We worship Your Son, **Your** Lamb, who purchased our redemption and brought us into Your fellowship. Make us a fit bride for our loving Groom.

The Lord's Marriage

Having seen how the Galileans went about the business of the wedding and God's marital relationship with His people Israel, let's start putting some things together. First, we need to acknowledge that customs are not Scripture, and Scripture is not bound to customs. However, Jesus' use of customs as illustrations, what He said, and what He did, **is** Scripture.

The Betrothal

Recall that the betrothal process was initiated by the father of the future groom. All the way back in Genesis the Father had a bride in view for the Son. Right away we have an issue between the custom and the spiritual reality. Who is the bride's father? Jesus said this to the religious Jews in John 8:44, *You are of your father the devil, and you want to do the desires of your father.* John also wrote this (1 John 3:10): *By this the children of God and the children of the devil are obvious: anyone who does not practice righteousness is not of God, nor the one who does not love his brother.* Now I cannot imagine that God had a sit-down with satan, much less invited that evil one to a big dinner to negotiate a marriage contract, but there was a bride price that had to be paid. Keep in mind that spiritual realities are not one dimensional. There are also other matters, like redemption and defeating satan, that Jesus accomplished by His death on the cross. That is why we cannot perfectly impose the customs on the reality.

I will insert here another part of the Galilean process that occurs prior to the betrothal, a cleansing process called *mikhveh*. The young couple, separately and at different times, would go to the synagogue. They stepped into a pool of water and scrunched down until the water covered their heads. When they stood up, they were considered to be clean and **born again**. This might add another dimension to both the Lord's and our baptism, but none of the New Testament writers addressed baptism in this context. However, our being washed by the water in the Word has plenty of mention. This is another cautionary example that custom cannot substitute for Scripture.

What is the bride price? Remember, the groom's father paid the bride price. Recall also that the wealthier the father, the more he was expected to pay. *For God so loved the world, that He gave His only begotten Son.* The God of the entire universe could not give more than His own Son. Anything less was not adequate.

Now we need a *ketubah*, the marriage contract. *This is My blood of the covenant* (Matthew 26:28 and Mark 14:24). By itself, this might be difficult to understand as a *ketubah*, but what Jesus said next places this covenant into its context.

But I say to you, I will not drink of this fruit of the vine from now on until that day when I drink it new with you in My Father's kingdom (Matthew 26:29). This is very similar to what the groom said to his bride in the Galilean custom. "You are now covenanted to me by the laws of Moses, and I will not drink of this cup again until I drink it anew with you in my father's house." Do you see two differences? The first is that Jesus said nothing about Moses. The second is that Jesus changed "in my father's house" to "in My Father's kingdom." I think this second difference is very significant. This is another dagger to both the homes-in-heaven thought and the idea that heaven is the Father's house. Jesus substituted "kingdom" for "house." The **kingdom** will be established on this earth. This will be discussed later.

In the Galilean custom the bride shows her acceptance of the marriage proposal by drinking from the cup of joy. The disciples did this by drinking from the cup that Jesus offered to them. This is recorded in Mark 14:23b. *He gave it to them, and they all drank from it.* Did they understand it in this way? The sources that I used all affirm this, saying that Jesus spoke often in a wedding context (more on this later), and that His statement about not drinking from the cup until He drinks again with them in the kingdom made the context perfectly clear. I can imagine them thinking, "This is a little weird," but they did not question. Drinking from the cup sealed the deal. We are betrothed to Christ!

During this betrothal period the Galilean couple would send gifts to each other. How is this realized today? We have received wonderful gifts from our Lord. Here is a short list.

Acts 10:45b - *because the gift of the Holy Spirit had been poured out on the Gentiles also.*
Romans 5:17b - *much more those who receive the abundance of grace and of the gift of righteousness*
Ephesians 2:8 - *For by grace you have been saved through faith; and that not of yourselves, it is the gift of God*
Ephesians 4:7 - *But to each one of us grace was given according to the measure of Christ's gift.*
Ephesians 4:8,11 - *and He gave gifts to men....And He gave some as apostles, and some as prophets, and some as evangelists, and some as pastors and teachers*

What about our part? What gifts can we give to our Groom? We can give only ourselves and what we have.

Philippians 4:18 - *having received from Epaphroditus what you have sent, a fragrant aroma, an acceptable sacrifice, well-pleasing to God.*
Romans 16:6 - *Greet Mary, who has worked hard for you.*
Hebrews 13:15 - *Through Him then, let us continually offer up a sacrifice of praise to God, that is, the fruit of lips that give thanks to His name.*
Psalm 116:12-13 - *What shall I render to the LORD For all His benefits toward me? I shall lift up the cup of salvation And call upon the name of the LORD.*

Being Ready

Now, what about the son building a room onto his father's house? If Jesus is not building us houses or rooms in heaven, then what is He doing? This is a critical part of the wedding story. The son could not get his bride until this part is completed. It had to be finished before his father would give his approval and allow his son to fetch the bride.

The traditional teaching, without a thought of the wedding, uses John 14 to say that Jesus is building stuff up in heaven. Those who do teach about the wedding use John 14 to tell us that when Jesus has completed His building project in heaven, the Father will tell Him to get His bride. If I have proved (remember John 14:29) that John 14 is not talking about that, then how do we fit in the wedding custom of the son building something?

In the context of the New Testament what is the Lord building? I hope that without hesitation, the answer is "the church." The relationship between Christ and the church is complex. We are sheep; He is the Shepherd. We are sinners; He is our Savior. We are His body; He is the Head. He is the vine; we are the branches. We are His bride; He is our Groom. We are the habitation of the living God. Christ is building us into something glorious and well-pleasing to the Father. At some point the Father will look at **us** and say, "Son, get Your bride!"

In saying this I have completely departed from **all** of the sources from whom I learned about the Galilean wedding. I better be able to show some scripture. I already have, but there is more.

Let's start with Revelation 6. After the fifth seal is broken John sees *the souls of those who had been slain because of the word of God, and because of the testimony which they had maintained* (verse 6:9). They cried to God for vengeance, and they wondered what was taking so long. God's answer is verse 11: *And there was given to each of them a white robe; and they were told that they should rest for a little while longer, until the number of their fellow servants and their brethren who were to be killed even as they had been, would be completed also.* The number will be completed. [Here i]It seems that a specific number of these martyrs is in view.

Now let us look at Ephesians 5:25-27. *Husbands, love your wives, just as Christ also loved the church and gave Himself up for her, so that He might sanctify her, having cleansed her by the washing of water with the word, that He might present to Himself the church in all her glory, having no spot or wrinkle or any such thing; but that she would be holy and blameless.* This speaks to our transformation. The Lord's shed blood has taken care of our sin problem, but our old nature remains to bother us. We are transformed by water, not by blood. This water comes to us by the Word, and I would say, not the written Word only, but also by the living word that the Holy Spirit speaks to us every day. Even as John 7:38 says, *He who believes in Me, as the Scripture said, 'From his innermost being will flow rivers of living water.'* This living water is for those **around** us, and **for** us. It washes away our spots (our cruddy nature) and removes our wrinkles (our oldness from the old creation), making us into a glorious church. Christ's church is wonderful, but we have no idea how glorious we can be! When this is completed, He will *present to Himself the church in all her glory.*

Here is a passage that must puzzle most, 2 Peter 3:11b-12a. I admit to being bothered by it in the past. *...what sort of people ought you to be in holy conduct and godliness, looking for and* **hastening** *the coming of the day of God.* How can we "hasten" that coming day? If we can understand that the Father is looking for some completeness in the church's expression and transformation, then it makes some sense. I have wasted a lot of time, even years, time that could have been used for my transformation. I have not only held myself back, but also the church. No wonder Hebrews 10:25 exhorts us to not forsake assembling together. It is much easier to run the race with others than alone. *And let us consider how to stimulate one another to love and good deeds, not forsaking our own assembling together, as is the habit of some, but encouraging one another; and all the more as you see the day drawing near* (Hebrews 10:24-25).

In Revelation 14 we see two harvests. The harvest of the grapes was destined for the "great winepress of the wrath of God" (verses 14:18-20). The other harvest, verses 14-16, is the harvest of God's people. They are removed before the wrath of God is poured out on the grapes. Note the second half of verse 15. *Put in your sickle and reap, for the hour to reap has come, because the harvest of the earth is ripe.* Today this harvest is not yet ripe, but one day it will be. We do not know the day, nor do we know the criteria for ripeness, but at some point the church will be ripe for this harvest.

Finally, we have Revelation 19:7. *Let us rejoice and be glad and give the glory to Him, for the marriage of the Lamb has come, and His bride has made herself ready.* This seems to parallel Ephesians 5, but in Ephesians the readiness is provided by the cleansing by the word provided by the Lord. Here verse 19:7 says that the bride has made **herself** ready. How? *It was given to her to clothe herself in fine linen, bright and clean; for the fine linen is the righteous acts of the saints* (verse 8). What are the righteous acts? In short, I would say acts of obedience. Hebrews 11 gives famous examples. John 14:21 (**not** speaking of the ten on stone tablets) says, *He who has My commandments and keeps them is the one who loves Me.* Chapter 2 of James has the familiar passage about faith that is living rather than dead (verse 2:14-26). He also said this in verse 1:25: *But one who looks intently at the perfect law, the law of liberty, and abides by it, not having become a forgetful hearer but an effectual doer, this man will be blessed in what he does.*

Compare those verses to Matthew 7:23. After the **lawless** ones make their claims to have done so many wonderful things in the Lord's name, He says that He never knew them. They claimed to have done all those wonderful things in the Lord's name, but He called them lawless.

The church in Sardis had many deeds to boast of, but they had not allowed the Lord to get to know them. The result was that they were dead, and they did not possess the white linen garments. But the Lord said that there were a few in Sardis *who have not soiled their garments; and they will walk with Me in white, for they are worthy* (Revelation 3:4). "But doesn't being washed in the blood of the Lamb make me worthy?" Not according to the Lord's word to Sardis.

While we might look at the world's degradation and look for signs of the Lord's return, the actual determining factor is the bride. God is like an orchestra conductor. Every group of instruments is coordinated by the conductor to arrive at the end of the piece in unison. The stringed instruments cannot get to the end before the brass section. The percussion section cannot lag behind. The conductor keeps everyone together. So it is with the approaching end of this age. The heavenly Conductor is keeping the world's economies, all the politics, and the church moving toward the end. The bride will be ready right on time.

The Wedding

The Galilean groom got his bride, and she was lifted in a chair and flown to the father's house. I do not try to hide details that are inconvenient. I face them and try to resolve them (unlike those who omit John 14:29 from their discussion, which is practically everyone). For those who want to hold on to the idea of heaven being God's house (despite my best efforts to dispel that), please remember three things. 1] Jesus said (Matthew 26:29), *But I say to you, I will not drink of this fruit of the vine from now on until that day when I drink it new with you in My Father's kingdom,* changing "in my father's house" to "in My Father's kingdom." 2] We **are** the building project. This is evident all through the New Testament. The idea of another building project in heaven is incongruent with God's New Testament economy, and it is not supported by any other scriptures. 3] John 14:28-29, the ignored verses.

What do we do with the custom of "flying the bride to the father's house"? The custom is not scripture, but we **are** going somewhere, as 1 Thessalonians 4:17 says. The problem is that traditional thought says two things that oppose each other. On one hand, it is said that Jesus is going to take us to our eternal home, and on the other that Jesus is returning to the earth to set up His kingdom. What are we doing up there if Jesus is down here? How can the bride be separated from her Husband? Are we not going to reign with Him in His kingdom? The "solution" is to say that heaven (the new Jerusalem) comes down to earth. However, since we **are** the new Jerusalem (see chapters 1 and 3 in this book), none of that holds water.

There **will** be a rapture. I am **not** in the camp that disagrees with that. Revelation 7:9 shows the great multitude standing before the throne and the Lamb, so clearly, we will be with the Father and the Lamb. However, at most we will be in heaven for seven years. Then we will return to the earth with the conquering Lord, as His wife(!), and reign with Him. This is seen in chapters 19, 21, and 22 of Revelation.

As for the rest of the Galilean custom, I am not sure how to chronologically apply some aspects of it. In the custom the newly-weds will keep to themselves for seven days, and the wedding feast will be in full swing simultaneously. If the seven years in heaven with our Groom equates to the couple in seclusion, I can surely see that. However, the kingdom age itself is referred to as the wedding feast (Revelation 19:9-11), and that **follows** the seven years. This is another example why the custom, while helpful, is not to be equated to scripture.

One thing to remember is that the wedding includes various parties: the groom, the bride, the bridesmaids, the best man, other friends of the groom, the parents, and the guests. Most of these are presented to us by Jesus in His parables (next chapter).

Children

Nearly all marriages produce children. This one is no different. Have I not offended you enough already? You can blame Paul. He was the one who broached this subject. He wrote that the Jerusalem above is our mother. In Galatians 4:22-31 He compared the children of bondage to the children of freedom, children of law to children of promise, children of the flesh to children of the Spirit. Here are verses 25-26: *Now this Hagar is Mount Sinai in Arabia and corresponds to the present Jerusalem, for she is in slavery with her children. But the Jerusalem above is free; she is our mother.*

How can Jerusalem above be our mother if it is a physical city? How can something with streets of gold and pearly gates be a mother? New Jerusalem can be our mother only if it is a spiritual entity. We have had a spiritual birth. That can result only from spiritual parents. As Jesus said, *That which is born of the flesh is flesh, and that which is born of the Spirit is spirit* (John 3:6). As has been demonstrated throughout this book, God's habitation is spiritual, the Lamb's bride is spiritual, and now we see that our mother is spiritual.

Practically speaking, the church gives birth to us. God's people preach the gospel and lead the lost to the Lord. Then the church nurtures them and raises them up. It does appear that the church is our mother. I hope that the case has already been made that the church (plus Old Testament saints) comprises the new Jerusalem. And so, we become a part of the church, a part of Jerusalem above, and a part of the mother that gives life to new believers.

This is why the author of Hebrews can say, *But you have come to Mount Zion and to the city of the living God,* **the heavenly Jerusalem,** *and to myriads of angels, to the general assembly and* **church of the firstborn** *who are enrolled in heaven, and to God, the Judge of all, and to the spirits of the righteous made perfect, and to Jesus, the mediator of a new covenant, and to the sprinkled blood, which speaks better than the blood of Abel* (Hebrews 12:22-24).

Just as God *made us alive together with Christ (by grace you have been saved), and raised us up with Him, and* **seated us with Him in the heavenly places** *in Christ Jesus* (Ephesians 2:5b-6), so also can Paul say that our mother is Jerusalem in heaven, even while the church is on earth.

In this book's second chapter, In The Beginning, we looked at events that parallel the New Testament, including the creation of Eve. Her name means "life" or "living." *Now the man called his wife's name Eve, because she was the mother of all the living* (Genesis 3:20). This is another parallel. Eve was the mother of all the living; the new Jerusalem is the mother of God's redeemed people.

In the Genesis 1:28 God said to Adam and Eve, *Be fruitful and multiply, and fill the earth, and subdue it; and rule over the fish of the sea and over the birds of the sky and over every living thing that moves on the earth.* The first couple failed to do that, so it remains for the second Couple. The need still exists. The last Adam and His last Eve have been very fruitful, and one day (maybe very soon) the holy Couple will indeed subdue the earth. Every earthly kingdom will be destroyed, and we will reign on the earth forever with our Husband. Everything that had its beginning in Genesis will find its completion and fulfillment in Revelation! God's marvelous plan will not be left undone; every detail will be completed. Let us be part of it!

Parables

Jesus used wedding scenarios in a few of His parables. I will cover them in their chronological order, not in the order that He spoke them. Before looking at the parables, however, how about we look at the wedding in John 2?

The Galilean Wedding

The first thing to notice is that the wedding in John 2 is a Galilean wedding! Jesus and His mother were invited, as well His disciples. The groom was easily accessible in verse 9, so this had to be after he and his bride had rejoined the feast. And that makes sense, because the wine would not have run out until later in the festivities.

Recall that the groom was responsible for getting everything prepared for the wedding feast. There had to be enough food and enough wine for the duration, a week or more. What embarrassment and shame the situation would have caused him! But Jesus saved the day, and the groom did not even know.

Because of verse 10, we know that Jesus does all things well, but I wonder what the headwaiter meant when he said, *Every man serves the good wine first, and when the people have drunk freely, then he serves the poorer wine; but you have kept the good wine until now.* To me it seems like a rebuke, but it could have been spoken with admiration. Either way, we can see in this statement that the groom was indeed the responsible party.

The things that distinguished the Galilean wedding from the Jewish are not evident in this account, but it surely is interesting that this was Jesus' first miracle.

The Ten Virgins

In the wedding custom the bride and her maids (*parthenos*, meaning "virgin") slept in their wedding clothes, and they made sure that they had plenty of oil for their lamps. The first parable of Matthew 25 is about ten of those bridesmaids. Since the groom usually comes at night, and this one in the parable did, they all were sleeping. Verse 6 says, *But at midnight there was a shout, "Behold, the bridegroom! Come out to meet him."* But now the problem becomes apparent. *For when the foolish took their lamps, they took no oil with them* (verse 3). The foolish ones asked the wise to share some of their oil. Nope. The five wise ones had to make sure that they had enough oil for the procession back to the father's house.

Now the foolish virgins were in a spot. They had to buy their oil, they but risked missing the wedding feast. They had no choice. By the time they bought the oil it was too late. The door was shut and there was no way to enter the wedding feast.

A key point is that the foolish virgins **did** buy the oil. The traditional teachings that they must not have been saved cannot be true. The unsaved cannot buy this oil. These virgins had hoped to get in the door, because now they had what they needed. The problem was being late. The consequence was missing the festivities.

Most of the Lord's parables and warnings are about this very thing: being in a position to participate in the joy of the Lord, but missing out due to unfaithfulness, laziness, and unwatchfulness. Are all these parables and warnings telling us how many ways the unsaved go to hell? No! The Lord is telling **believers** how many ways **we** can miss the enjoyment of the wedding! Consider what the Lord said to the Laodicean church. He advised them to buy gold refined by fire, white garments and eye salve (Revelation 3:18). Those who do, those who overcome, will sit with Him on His throne. Those who do not buy the necessary things will be spit out of His mouth. What does that mean? Does anyone address that (without saying that they lost their salvation or never were saved)? We can look around and we can look at ourselves. Have we never seen lukewarmness in God's people?

It is not the purpose of this book to go deeply into that topic; it was covered thoroughly in *RYR*. The point of the parable is that Jesus used the context of a wedding to make the case for our being prepared for His coming. Let us take the warning.

Come to the Feast

In Matthew 22 we have another wedding feast. Many had been invited to the feast (verse 3), but when the big day came, they preferred not to go. How insulting! Maybe there was a big game on TV. Oh, verse 5 says that many were working. Kidding aside, verses 6 and 7 show that Jesus was referring to the Jews. *And the rest seized his slaves and mistreated them and killed them. But the king was enraged, and he sent his armies and destroyed those murderers and set their city on fire.* So then, the king sent his slaves to find whomever they could, wherever they could. That did the trick; the wedding feast was packed.

But, alas, one was found who did not belong. According to the wedding custom the guests were provided with white garments when they arrived. The white garments served two functions. The garments showed that the guests were honored. They also prevented wedding crashers, who might have been looking for the best meal that they would see in a year. People were poor, and life was hard, so hunger was a companion to many. This guy didn't have a wedding garment, so he was expelled.

Who are these guests? I think they are taken from the nations, from among unregenerated gentiles. Most will say that these guests are us. I think not. This is discussed in the next chapter.

One thing I realized when I started working on this book is that there are no parables about the bride. She is not mentioned even in the parable of the ten virgins. Maybe those who constitute the bride do not need a warning.

The parables are for the bridesmaids and the guests. Hmmm, interesting. The bridesmaids are close to the bride, but they are not the bride. The guests join the celebration, but they are not part of the wedding party. The next chapter will get into these details.

But first…

After the Feast

There is one more parable, and chronologically it is the last. Well, I think it is the last. Luke 12:36 says this: *Be like men who are waiting for their master when he returns **from the wedding feast**.* That statement has always troubled me from the time I started paying attention to the parables. The other parables are clearly pre-wedding feast in their setting. They warn us to be ready so that we can enter into the enjoyment. But this parable features those who were not at the wedding, and we are told that **they** need to be in a state of watchfulness when the master returns from it.

In *RYR* I mentioned this parable in the discussion of the parable of the ten virgins in Matthew because this parable in verse 12:35 begins with *Be dressed in readiness, and keep your lamps lit.* But there is more to it.

Here is the parable, verses 35-38. *Be dressed in readiness, and keep your lamps lit. Be like men who are waiting for their master when he returns from the wedding feast, so that they may immediately open the door to him when he comes and knocks. Blessed are those slaves whom the master will find on the alert when he comes; truly I say to you, that he will gird himself to serve, and have them recline at the table, and will come up and wait on them. Whether he comes in the second watch, or even in the third, and finds them so, blessed are those slaves.*

This parable seems to confirm what I wrote in *RYR*. In the Conclusion chapter I wrote this:

> Therefore, I see two conclusions for us who have been saved but have not allowed the Lord to lead us into full salvation: (A) either enduring the tribulation, or some portion of it; or (B) spending a good part (if not the whole) of the next age, the kingdom age, in an unpleasant situation.
>
> I think it primarily depends on whether we are alive at the end of this age, when the Lord gathers the faithful (Philadelphia vs Laodicea), or whether we are already passed from this life.

The Lord, of course, will sort it all out, but the warnings are clearly before us.

This parable in Luke 12 fits scenario B, "spending a good part (if not the whole) of the next age, the kingdom age, in an unpleasant situation." In the parable in Luke 12 the master is coming to those who had been shut out. Will they yet be unwatchful?

I have assumed that the two scenarios would remedy whatever kept us from allowing the Lord to gain our whole heart, but apparently that is not true. Am I over thinking this? I hope I am, but Jesus is the One who spoke the parable. Why did He mention returning "from the wedding feast"? Has anyone ever given a message that included the four words "from the wedding feast"? After reading the verses to begin a sermon, has anyone discussed what those four words might mean? The church has a tendency to ignore words that are inconvenient or do not fit traditional teaching (John 14:28-29, Revelation 3:5). The Lord fetches His bride, and **then** the wedding takes place. The other parables described above fit that bill. This one cannot be a parable about the rapture since it is post-wedding. This parable would have to be placed sometime after that, after the wedding feast, a thousand years later.

The good news is that even these slaves, if they have been watchful, will be served by the Lord. What mercy!

Who's Who?

There are five parties identified as participants in a wedding: the groom, the best man (the friend of the bridegroom), the bride, the bridesmaids, and the guests. The Groom is easily identified as Jesus, and John the Baptist is the best man (see John 3:29). I do not know whether he will have a role in the future.

Who comprise the other parties? I will first identify the guests. From the parable of the sheep and goats in Matthew 25 the guests will be the sheep, those who helped God's people. These people are not part of the wedding party, but they will enjoy the celebration of the next age. And since I think these are the guests, I believe that the parable about the wedding guests are these. That could explain the harsh treatment of the one who was tossed out of the feast; he was actually a goat.

It is more difficult to distinguish between those who constitute the bride and those who are the bridesmaids. I am convinced that **not all** of us (Christians in the true sense) will constitute the bride. If all of us make up the bride, then who will be the bridesmaids? It is clear from the parable in Matthew 25 that the bridesmaids have the Spirit, but nevertheless, they are not the bride.

Who will constitute the bride and who will be bridesmaids? I am not going to claim any insight into this. I do not know. There might be an indication in the letter to the church in Philadelphia. Revelation 3:12 says, *He who overcomes, I will make him a pillar in the temple of My God, and he will not go out from it anymore; and I will write on him the name of My God, and the name of the city of My God,* **the new Jerusalem***, which comes down out of heaven from My God, and My new name.* Those who overcome the degradation of the church wherever they are will have three names written upon him: God, Christ's new name, and the new Jerusalem. God, the Lamb, and the bride. Also, overcomers will rule with Christ, even Laodiceans (Revelation 2:27 and 3:21).

What's left for the bridesmaids? I do not know. Perhaps the bridesmaids become melded in with the bride. I am still asking, seeking, and knocking about that one. As I wrote earlier, there are no parables for the bride, but there is the one for the bridesmaids. Whether or not I am privileged to be part of the bride, I need to heed that parable. With my history, I will be quite joyous in being a bridesmaid who gets in before the door is shut.

The Nations

Please understand that there will be nations. *The **nations** will walk by its light, and the kings of the earth will bring their glory into it* (Revelation 21:24).

There will be kings. Who are they? I hope you know that they will be from among us. *He who overcomes, and he who keeps My deeds until the end, to him I will give authority over the nations; and he shall rule them with a rod of iron* (Revelation 2:26-27a). *He who overcomes, I will grant to him to sit down with Me on My throne, as I also overcame and sat down with My Father on His throne* (Revelation 3:21). See the parables of the faithful and unfaithful servants in Matthew 25:14-30 and Luke 19:11-26.

If we are the kings, then who are the nations? We cannot be the nations, ruling (shepherding) as kings over ourselves! With a rod of iron?

There is a well known parable in Matthew 25 about sheep and goats. Here are verses 31 and 32a. *But when the Son of Man comes in His glory, and all the angels with Him, then He will sit on His glorious throne. All the nations will be gathered before Him.* What is the first word? The first word is "but." This parable is being contrasted against the parable that preceded it. What is the contrast? The parable in Matthew 25:14-30 is about the Lord distributing talents to His slaves. The issue is faithfulness vs unfaithfulness. That parable begins at verse 14 with the words "for it is just like." That makes the parable similar to the one that preceded **it**, the parable of the virgins. The issue with the virgins was being wise or unwise. So, the first two parables of chapter 25 have similar themes. They concern the Lord's dealings with His own when He judges us at His *bema* seat. As 2 Corinthians 5:10 says, *For we must all appear before the judgment seat of Christ, so that each one may be recompensed for his deeds in the body, according to what he has done, whether good or bad.*

Then we come to the third parable (sheep and goats), and it begins "but." What is the contrast? In this parable it is not we who are being judged, but the nations. This is **after** the Lord's dealings with us. Now He has come in His glory, and He has set up His kingdom on this earth. He gathers the nations before His throne, and then a separation happens. The criteria are quite clear in verses 35 and 36. *For I was hungry, and you gave Me something to eat; I was thirsty, and you gave Me something to drink; I was a stranger, and you invited Me in; naked, and you clothed Me; I was sick, and you visited Me; I was in prison, and you came to Me.* Those that the King had placed to His right, the sheep, are quite surprised at this development. "Wait, what? When did we do that?"

At the time of the Lord's setting up His kingdom, the people who had survived the tribulation are being evaluated on what they did to help God's people, probably especially during that time. If they provided support or aid in some way, they are considered to be sheep. I believe that these will be among the guests of the wedding feast. If they did nothing for God's people, then they are placed on the King's left and considered as goats. They are sent *into the eternal fire which has been prepared for the devil and his angels* (verse 25:41). These guys don't even make it to the great white throne judgment, which is a thousand years later.

I have heard Bible teachers make this parable about us. If your idea of eternity is mansions in heaven and walking on streets of gold, with no thought of Christ's kingdom on this earth, then that is about all you can do. We, the sheep, go to heaven; the rest go to hell. Concerning this parable, they have to contort Jesus' clear speaking into something like this: "If we are Christians, then we are going to love Jesus for everything that He did for us. This love should express itself in feeding the poor, visiting those in prison, etc. In doing these things out of love, we are actually not saved by works, because we were saved by grace to start with." Then what was the point to the parable? Jesus' clear speaking is lost.

I also suggest that maybe others will join these as the earth's inhabitants after the millennium. Notice Revelation 20:15. *And if anyone's name was not found written in the book of life, he was thrown into the lake of fire.* Did you see the word "if"? Our assumption is that "if" does not mean "if;" but that it means everyone. But it does not say "everyone." They will be judged "according to their deeds." Maybe those deeds include helping God's people, let's say during WWII or during other repressive regimes. I do not know, but the possibility seems to be there if we take the Word as it is written.

The Habitation of God

One of the main reasons that I am so passionate about John 14 is that I want to change our thinking about who benefits from the abiding. Surely we benefit, but in the two verses where the Greek word *mone* is used, we are looking at God's dwelling. In verse 2 the **Father's** house has many abodes, and in verse 23 those abodes are us. It is God's house that is being built, not ours.

In chapter 15 Jesus mentions abiding ten times, saying that we need to abide in Him and that we need to allow Him (and His words) to abide in us. In chapter 14 *mone* is a noun; in chapter 15 *meno* is a verb. *Meno* is the verb form of *mone*. The beneficiary of this abiding is God; *My Father is glorified by this, that you bear much fruit, and so prove to be My disciples* (verse 15:8). Yes, we also benefit. God is not selfish: *These things I have spoken to you so that My joy may be in you, and that your joy may be made full* (verse 11). But all things are for God.

It is fair to wonder why this chapter about God's habitation is in a book about the new Jerusalem. We are many things to God and to His Christ. I mentioned before that this relationship is complicated. We are the body of Christ and the branches of the vine, we are His brothers, we are the house of God, we are the house**hold** of God, and we are the bride. We are the building project of the Son, who is waiting for approval of the Father. In this chapter we will look at God's house in the epistles and (saving the best for last) Revelation.

In Corinthians

In 1 Corinthian 3 Paul writes in verse 10 that *according to the grace of God which was given to me, like a wise master builder I laid a foundation, and another is building on it.* He also talks about us participating in the building in verse 12. *Now if any man builds on the foundation...* This shows a process that has continued from the early church until now. It will not stop until the end of this age.

Just a few verses down Paul explains that even though the building is an active process, we already are God's temple. Here are verses 16 and 17. *Do you not know that **you are** a temple of God and that the Spirit of God dwells in you? If any man destroys the temple of God, God will destroy him, for the temple of God is holy, and that is what **you are**.* The "you" in both verses is plural, so Paul is referring to the church. We are building something in spirit, but we already are a spiritual temple.

In 2 Corinthians Paul tells us what it means to be God's temple. Here are verses 6:16b and 18. *For we are the temple of the living God; just as God said, "I will dwell in them and walk among them, and I will be their God, and they shall be my people. ... And I will be a father to you, and you shall be sons and daughters to Me," says the Lord Almighty.* Paul is taking scripture from Exodus 25:8, Exodus 29:45-46, and Leviticus 26:12, but changed the idea that God would dwell **among** the Israelites to the New Testament reality that God will dwell **in** us. And verse 18 (back to 2 Corinthians) continues by saying that He will be our Father! This is what it means to be God's temple! He will dwell in us, and He will be our Father! Why does this remind me of John 14?!

<u>In Ephesians</u>

We can see several aspects of our relationship with God coming together in Ephesians 2:19-22. *So then you are no longer strangers and aliens, but you are fellow **citizens** with the saints, and are of God's **household**, having been **built** on the foundation of the apostles and prophets, Christ Jesus Himself being the corner stone, in whom the whole **building**, being fitted together, is growing into a holy **temple** in the Lord, in whom you also are being built together into a **dwelling** of God in the Spirit.* We are fellow citizens with the saints and part of God's household because we were added to the building. This building is a living building! It is **growing** into a living temple in the Lord. And, in the Lord we are being built together into a dwelling place of God. That sure is a mouthful! Did I say that our relationship with God is complicated? Only Paul,

God's chosen vessel, could have such a wondrous thought. Of course, it was by the Holy Spirit, but Paul was a gift to the church. All of this is to produce the bride, the new Jerusalem.

In Hebrews

Hebrews gives us two references to God's house. Verse 3:6 says, *but Christ was faithful as a Son over His house—whose house we are, if we hold fast our confidence and the boast of our hope firm until the end.* The antecedent for "His" seems to be God from verse 4. Verse 10:21 says, *and since we have a great priest over the house of God.* This verse says that the Son is the great high Priest over God's house (which house we are).

In verse 3:6 notice the attached condition: *if we hold fast our confidence and the boast of our hope firm until the end.* This seems to align with the parables that we looked at.

In 1 Peter

Of the eleven original apostles only Peter and John have letters included in the New Testament. It is interesting to me to see things that Jesus said reflected in their letters. Jesus told Peter that he is a stone. At that moment Jesus also told Peter that He was going to build His church (Matthew 16:18). In his second letter Peter says that we *as living stones, are being built up as a spiritual house* (1 Peter 2:5). As we know already, the church is this spiritual house.

God's house, the Father's house, is living and spiritual. It is not physical. No one can point to it and say, "there it is." God's house is physical only in the sense that we ourselves are physical. But eventually, these physical bodies will be replaced with spiritual bodies, just like the Lord's. We will be seen and touchable, but quite spiritual, as Paul said in 1 Corinthians 15:44. *It is sown a natural body, it is raised a spiritual body. If there is a natural body, there is also a spiritual body.*

In Revelation

We have already seen the vision of the bride in Revelation. There is another thing to see, and I really did save the best for last. If you have read *RYR* this should not be new. Remember that I have said several times that as it is now, so it will always be.

In chapter 21 we see a new heaven and a new earth. Verse 2 says this, *And I saw the holy city, new Jerusalem, coming down out of heaven from God, made ready as a bride adorned for her husband.* The bride, new Jerusalem, is coming to the earth. On this earth are nations that have been permitted to live in and enjoy the kingdom. If you need help to understand the nations, please read again the previous chapter.

With this as background, read verse 21:3a. *And I heard a loud voice from the throne, saying, "Behold, the tabernacle of God is among men..."* How is that traditionally understood? My thought was that God's tabernacle has come here to be with us. That is easy to understand, right? But, if **we** are the tabernacle, if we **are** the tabernacle, then how can that change our understanding?

We, the bride, the city of God, the body of Christ, the tabernacle of God, come down to the earth after our marriage to the Lamb. **We** will be among the nations, even as the church is now! Today the church is among people. The bride, which is the tabernacle of God, will be among the people. As it is now, so it will always be, only better! We will be their shepherds, bringing life to them.

And He will dwell among them, and they shall be His people, and God Himself will be among them (verse 21:3b). In us and through us God will be among the inhabitants of the earth. Our flesh will no longer hinder God's expression through us. The world will no longer see our shortcomings; there will not be any! We will be thoroughly transformed and transparent even as John described the holy city.

And He will wipe away every tear from their eyes; and there will no longer be any death; there will no longer be any mourning, or crying, or pain; the first things have passed away (verse 21:4). We think this verse applies to us, but verse 4 is a continuation of verse

3. The "loud voice from the throne" is still talking about the people among whom the tabernacle has come. These people will have just gone through the years of famine, heat, judgments, and the last war of the great tribulation. They will need our comfort, and we will teach them about God and His law. They will be "His people," and through us "God Himself will be among them."

Does that not sound comforting, compassionate, and caring? These people will be free to live a full human life while receiving our shepherding. (By "full," I am referring to quality of life, not duration. There will be no more death.) These are the nations mentioned in Revelation 21 and 22. [To be thorough, there is a reference to wiping away tears that does have application to some of us. In Revelation 7 (verses 14 and 17), in describing those who had "come out of the great tribulation," an elder said to John that "God will wipe every tear from their eyes." We have to be aware of context when we talk about things here and there.]

God's habitation, His house, has always been the means by which He dwells with man and with His chosen people specifically. In the Old Testament God's house was a physical structure. He did not intend for that to be His home forever. The tabernacle in the wilderness was obviously temporary, but even the temple was not where His heart was. It was aloof in a manner of speaking. The Holy Place was accessible for only certain members of the priesthood, and the Holiest Place could be entered by only the High Priest, and on only one day of the year, the Day of Atonement.

When Jesus died on the cross, the veil that kept the Holiest Place hidden was torn from top to bottom. Now God was free to leave the place in which he had confined Himself and enter into the hearts of people! Hallelujah!

God's heart is, and always was, on the bride for His Son, and the bride herself is God's habitation. This discussion will be concluded at the end of the next chapter.

The Spirit and the Bride

I know more than one person who reads the last chapter of a nonfiction work to see what the rest of the book is about. In case that is you, I will try to fulfill your aim.

That strategy also works for God's Word. The end of the Bible shows us the bride. It might be that some are surprised that I see the grand marriage of the Son and His bride as the purpose of God's work in creation. Traditional thought is that God's plan culminates in our going to heaven and living in comfortable mansions in a huge city with streets made of gold. I hope that this book totally demolished all that for you. That concept makes God's eternal purpose all about us. Even while allowing that God wants to have fellowship with man, that realization seems to take a back seat to the fulfillment of our desires.

One Spirit

God certainly wants fellowship with man, but the Bible shows us that He wants a fellowship so intimate that only marriage can describe it. Only marriage can fulfill it. After Adam's declaration that Eve was bone of his bones and flesh of his flesh, God said (Genesis 2:24), *For this reason a man shall leave his father and his mother, and be joined to his wife; and they shall become one flesh.* What does the New Testament say? Here is 1 Corinthians 6:17: *But the one who joins himself to the Lord is **one spirit** with Him.* "With Him" is italicized in Bibles; it does not appear in the original text. The verse actually reads, *But the one who joins himself to the Lord is **one spirit**.* "One flesh" is according to the old creation, and "one spirit" is according to the new, even according to the new covenant. In the old creation flesh is joined to flesh, but in the new creation Spirit is joined to spirit. Our human spirit is enlivened by God's Spirit, the Holy Spirit, and we are made one spirit with our Groom, our Husband. What intimacy!

From Genesis to Revelation there are indications, hints, clues, and outright declarations that the Father is building a bride for His Son. Just as God built Eve from Adam and they became one flesh, God is building the church from out of Christ. He and we are one spirit. How beautiful is that?!

Beautiful, Colorful

In this book I have said a few times that our relationship with God is complicated. That was for simplicity. It might be better to say that our relationship with God is a variety of colors!

Paul wrote to the Ephesians that *the manifold wisdom of God might now be made known through the church* (Ephesians 3:10). The Greek word for "manifold" is *polypoikilos*. This word suggests greatly varied, especially a great variety of colors. God's wisdom is colorful! This wisdom is displayed in us, showing all the wonderful colors of God in and through His people. We all are different shades of Jesus, and we display the varied colors of His salvation. This is the new Jerusalem, such a colorful and beautiful city!

In saying that God's big plan is for a wedding does not diminish any of those other aspects of our relationship to Him. God is big enough and pure enough for all those other realities to be true, while keeping the end in view. His love for us is genuine. He gave His only begotten Son because He loves the world. He desires that all would be saved. No matter if our role in the next age is the least in the kingdom, it will be infinitely better than eternity without God. (See Psalm 84:10.)

Creation is for this Marriage

Nevertheless, all human history has been for producing the bride, from Adam and Eve in the garden to the worst days of the coming tribulation. Isaiah 24 is a foreboding chapter, but at the end, verse 23b says, *for the LORD of hosts will reign on Mount Zion and in Jerusalem.* His bride will reign with Him. She will cover the earth, ministering to the people and shepherding them.

At the end of chapter 5, Betrothal, there is a list of resources for some of the information that I gleaned for this book. Jay McCarl is one of them. He has a video, which is listed there, in which he depicts a Galilean betrothal. I recommend that you watch it. Just after the one hour and eighteen minute mark he said this (printed with Jay's permission):

> That's the purpose for which God made the universe. It's the purpose for which the fall of man occurred and the redemption of man through Christ came, because He did all of this to bring a bride to Himself for all eternity.

I agree with that. God's story with man ends with the bride. All of creation and all of history has been for this marriage! *Then I heard something like the voice of a great multitude and like the sound of many waters and like the sound of mighty peals of thunder, saying, "Hallelujah! For the Lord our God, the Almighty, reigns. Let us rejoice and be glad and give the glory to Him, for the marriage of the Lamb has come and His bride has made herself ready"* (Revelation 19:6-7). Even though the written story ends there, this is only the beginning. The divine couple will be together for all eternity!

I beg you, please forget about the songs that tell of mansions, distant shores, pearly gates, etcetera, etcetera. What God has planned is far more glorious than the best that those other things could ever be. It is also more real. We will have spiritual bodies, living as spiritual people, yet physical, just as our Lord did after His resurrection. We will be on this earth as portrayed in the last two chapters of the Bible and as promised by God through His prophets. Do you think the wolf (not the lion) will dwell with the lamb in heaven? No! They are earthly creatures, and they will live on a renewed earth. (See Isaiah 11:6 and 65:25)

Likewise, man was always meant for the earth. The bride (new Jerusalem) comes down out of heaven to the earth because her

Husband comes to the earth. This is where His kingdom will be. He will sit on the throne of David, and we will be with Him. We will not be in heaven, separated from Him.

The Water of Life

When we get to the last chapter of Revelation, John gives us an epilog in verses 22:18-21. Just prior to that we have the final words from Jesus and Someone else. Here is verse 16. *I, Jesus, have sent My angel to testify to you these things for the churches. I am the root and the descendant of David, the bright morning star.* Then verse 17: *The Spirit and the bride say, "Come." And let the one who hears say, "Come." And let the one who is thirsty come; let the one who wishes take the water of life without cost.*

Why did the speaking change from Jesus in verse 16 to the Spirit in verse 17? Why doesn't verse 17 say "Jesus and the bride" or "the Lamb and the bride"? From Genesis 1:1 until now we can see God working in His one-threeness throughout history. Our triune God created all things. Our triune God made Adam and built Eve. It was Jehovah, I AM, who said that He was a husband to the Israelite nation (Jeremiah 31:32). Our triune God worked in history to point all things to the cross. Our triune God is working in resurrection to build the church, resulting in the bride.

Now we see our triune God speaking in Revelation. Just as the last Adam became a life-giving Spirit, He will always be the life-giving Spirit! The river of life flows from the throne, even from our spirit, to reach humanity today. Today the bride is one with her Husband and one with the Spirit in speaking a simple, yet profound invitation. *Let the one who is thirsty come; let the one who wishes take the water of life without cost.*

Take the water of life. This is how it begins....for all of us. The Spirit and the bride are working together to bring sinners to the Son. From this initial salvation and through renewing and transformation we somehow, marvelously, become a glorious bride. Wow! Only God can pull this off!

Thank You, Father! Thank You, Jesus! Thank You, Holy Spirit!

The Heart of the Bible

The heart of the Bible is whatever has the highest priority in God's heart. Heaven is not the heart of the Bible. Going to heaven is not the heart of the Bible. Even our salvation is not the heart of the Bible. God's heart is centered on a bride for the Son, and together the holy couple will lovingly shepherd humanity on this earth. The expression of God will be unhindered and full of glory!

Earlier in this book I quoted Jeremiah 31:31-32 and said that these verses are a microcosm of Israel's history in one sentence. There is a comparable statement in the New Testament. *Husbands, love your wives, just as Christ also loved the church and gave Himself up for her, so that He might sanctify her, having cleansed her by the washing of water with the word, that He might present to Himself the church in all her **glory**, having no spot or wrinkle or any such thing; but that she would be holy and blameless* (Ephesians 5:25-27). Let's break this down.

- Christ loved the church and gave Himself up for her. That is the cross.
- He is cleansing her by the washing of the water in the Word. This Word is not *logos*, the written Word; it is *rhema*, the Word that writes on our hearts. It might be the *rhema* that speaks to us as we read the *logos*, and it might be the Spirit's guidance as we go about our lives.
- So that He might sanctify her. The washing results in our sanctification, our being set apart for our Groom. This is dispositional.
- That He might present her to Himself in all her glory. "Son, go get Your bride!" She is glorious! She is holy!

Yes, I consider John 14 to be the heart of the Bible, but John 14 is for this. John 14 is for the bride. Everything is for the bride! God left the man-made temple so that we could become the bride. He is making His home in our hearts so that we can become the bride. He comes to us in His one-threeness so that the bride can be built up.

This is why we run our race. This is what is on God's heart. This is the heart of the Bible.

I hope that you have seen something. I hope that your heart has been stirred. Time appears to be in short supply. This age seems to be spiraling downward. May we align our hearts with God. Let us hasten the day and become the bride made ready!

Let us rejoice and be glad and give the glory to Him, for the marriage of the Lamb has come and His bride has made herself ready.

Scripture Index

Genesis
1:27	5
1:28	69
2:4	5
2:18	5,6,7
2:19	6
2:20	5-6,7
2:21	6
2:22	6
2:23	6
2:24	87
3:20	69
15:4-5	48
15:6	48
15:7	49
15:8	49
15:17-18	49
15:18	58

Exodus
19:3	47
23:20-33	48
24:4	47
24:12	47-48
25:8	82
29:45-46	82
31:18	48
32:1	50
32:5	50
32:6	50
32:13	50
32:15	48

Leviticus
26:12	82

Judges
2:17	49

1 Samuel
2:20	29

1 Kings
8:30,39,43	29

1 Chronicles
17:12	30

2 Chronicles
25:10	29
36:23	29

Psalms
84:10	88
103:19	29
116:12-13	63
123:1	29

Isaiah
2:2-3	20
11:6	89
24:23	88-89
54:5-8	52
54:11-12	22
56:7	30
60:1-3	16
60:11	22
60:14	22
60:19	22
65:17	22
65:25	89
66:1	29

Jeremiah
3:8	51
3:10	51
12:7	30
31:31	57
31:31-32	47,91
31:32	57,90
31:33	57
34:18	49

Ezekiel
9:3	51
10:4	51-52
10:18	52
10:19	52
11:23	52
23:39	30
36:26-27	57-58
47:9	22
48:30-34	22

Hosea
2:2	51
2:13	53
2:14	52
2:16	52

Micah
4:1-2	20
4:2	21

Zechariah
1:16	30
14:16	21
14:16-17	20-21

Matthew
5:14	14
7:23	66
7:24	27
10:13	27
16:18	7,9,83
21:19	19
22:3	73
22:5	73
22:6-7	73
24:32-35	19
25:3	72
25:6	72
25:14-30	77
25:31-32	77
25:35-36	78
25:41	78

26:28	62	13:38-14:1	26,34	5:17	63
26:29	62,67	14:1-3	38	7:2	55
Mark		14:2	6,27,28	7:3	55
3:25	27		30,31,33	7:4	18,55-56
11:13	19		35,81		57
13:28-31	19	14:2-3	31,32,38	8:2	57
14:23	62	14:3	33,35	8:29	32,35
14:24	62		36,37	16:6	63
16:14	37	14:3-5	33		
		14:6	33,34,35	**1 Corinthians**	
		14:7	34	2:9	iii
Luke		14:9-11	34	2:10	iii
12:35	74	14:16	35	2:12-13	iii
12:36	74	14:17	34	3:9	7,9
12:35-38	74	14:18	35,36	3:10	81
13:6-9	19	14:20	35	3:12	81
19:9	27	14:21	66	3:16-17	82
19:11-26	77	14:23	31,35	3:17	30,33
22:54	28		36,81	6:18	82
24:41	37	14:27	36	6:17	87
		14:27-29	38	12:12	33
John		14:28	31,36,37	12:27	33
1:14	32,35	14:28-29	33,36	15:44	83
2:9	71		38,67,75	16:15	27
2:10	71	14:29	31,36		
2:19	9		38,64,67	**2 Corinthians**	
2:21	9	15:5	iii,17	5:10	77
3:6	68	15:8	81	6:16	30,82
3:16	62	15:11	81	6:18	82
3:29	75	19:34	7	11:2	7
4:10	16,33	20:17	37		
4:14	16,33	20:19	37	**Galatians**	
4:36	18	20:20	37	3:7	55
7:37-38	17	20:22	25,35	3:13	55
7:38	33,65		36-37,37	3:14	55
8:12	14			3:17	58
8:44	61	**Acts**		3:24	20
9:5	14	2:36	28	4:22-31	68
11:20	28	10:2	28	4:24	11
12:24	32,33	10:45	63	4:25-26	68
12:46	14	20:28-31	15	5:22-23	18
13:18-19	31			**Ephesians**	
13:33	26	**Romans**		2:5	56,57
13:36-38	26	4:13	58	2:5-6	69
13:38	36	4:16	58	2:8	63

2:18	34	James		19:15	21	
2:19-22	82	1:25	57,64	20:15	78,79	
2:21-22	7,9,30,33	2:14-26	66	21:2	3,4,8,84	
2:22	32			21:3	84	
3:10	88	1 Peter		21:4	84	
4:7	63	2:5	8,83	21:9	iii,3,4,12	
4:8	63				23	
4:11	63	2 Peter		21:9-10	12,23	
4:12	9	1:2-3	8-9	21:10	3,4	
4:16	9	1:4	9	21:11	13	
5:8-9	18	3:11-12	13,65	21:12-14	14	
5:23	7			21:21	16	
5:25-26	7,8	1 John		21:22	22	
5:25-27	64-65,91	3:10	61	21:24	15,16	
5:27	7,65				19,77	
5:29-30	7	Jude		21:25	15	
5:32	8	1:12	21	21:26	15-16,19	
				21:27	15	
Philippians		Revelation		22:1	16	
1:6	9	1:4	15	22:2	17,18,19	
2:15	13	1:12	11	22:14	17-18	
4:18	63	1:20	12	22:15	15	
4:22	27	2:26-27	77	22:16	90	
		2:27	76	22:17	90	
Colossians		3:4	66	22:18-21	90	
2:17	11	3:5	75			
		3:12	3,76			
1 Thessalonians		3:18	72			
4:17	67	3:21	76,77			
		5:5-6	4			
1 Timothy		6:9	64			
3:15	28,30	6:11	64			
		7:9	67			
Hebrews		7:14	85			
3:6	28,83	7:17	85			
8:8-9	56	14:14-16	65			
8:13	56	14:18-20	65			
10:1	11	17:2-6	12			
10:21	83	17:18	12			
10:24-25	65	19:1-4	12			
12:2	9	19:6-7	13,89			
12:11	18	19:7	66,92			
12:22-24	69	19:[7-]8	66			
13:15	63	19:9-11	68			
		19:11	13			

www.ingramcontent.com/pod-product-compliance
Lightning Source LLC
Chambersburg PA
CBHW070526030426
42337CB00016B/2120